A PRACTICAL GUIDE TO POSTGRADUATE
RESEARCH IN THE BUSINESS AREA

GW00691975

ABOUT THE AUTHORS

Frédéric Adam, Dip ISCP, MBS, PhD, is a college lecturer in the Department of Accounting, Finance and Information Systems in University College Cork in Ireland. He is also a senior researcher with the Executive Systems Research Centre. He holds a Ph.D. from the National University of Ireland (NUI) and Université Paris VI jointly. His research has been published in a number of international journals, including the Journal of Strategic Information Systems, Decision Support Systems and Systèmes d'Information et Management. He has also co-edited *A Manager's Guide to Current Issues in Information Systems* (Blackhall Publishing, 1999). He also acts regularly as a consultant in the areas of information systems implementation and information systems for top managers.

Margaret Healy, BComm, ACMA, MBS, is a college lecturer with the Department of Accounting, Finance and Information Systems, University College Cork, Ireland. Subsequent to obtaining her primary degree, she worked for a number of years with a major international Irish food ingredients company as a Management Accountant. She came back to UCC in 1994 where she submitted an MBS thesis on Business Process Engineering. She is currently working on a doctoral thesis investigating capital investment systems in high-technology industries.

They are the creators and the directors of the Master of Business Studies in Management Information and Managerial Accounting Systems at University College Cork, a two year programme which includes traditional exams, a six month industrial placement and a minor dissertation. As such, they have considerable up to date experience in administering postgraduate studies and supervising postgraduate work.

A Practical Guide to Postgraduate Research in the Business Area: Coping with Pandora's Box

Frédéric Adam and
Margaret Healy

BLACKHALL
Publishing

This book was typeset by GOUGH TYPESETTING SERVICES for

BLACKHALL PUBLISHING
8 Priory Hall
Stillorgan, Co. Dublin
Ireland

e-mail: blackhall@eircom.net
www.blackhallpublishing.com

ISBN: 1 901657 98 1

A catalogue record for this book is available from the British Library.

Printed in Ireland by
ColourBooks

Contents

PART TWO: COPING WITH PANDORA'S BOX

Acknowledgements

This book is the result of a concerted effort between two colleagues at University College Cork who spend much of their time supervising and working with postgraduate students. We are both co-directors of a Masters of Business Studies programme, which we contributed to designing a few years ago. This book was therefore developed as an essential text for the dissertation element of this degree. It is naturally based on the experience we have accumulated as co-directors of this programme, as well as in our own individual research odysseys.

However, many sincere thanks are due to the other contributors to this work – the dozens of colleagues and friends with whom we have ongoing discussions about the issue of postgraduate supervision and research in general. In this long list, a number of individuals deserve a special mention: Tom Butler, Eleanor Doyle, Pat Finnegan, Brian Fitzgerald, Ella Kavanagh, Ciaran Murphy, Colin McCormac and Ted O'Leary from University College Cork; Jean-Charles Pomerol from Université Pierre et Marie Curie (Paris 6) et Jean-Claude Courbon from the Institut National des Télécommunications (Evry, France).

It would be foolish to ignore or deny the enormous contribution of the numerous postgraduate students we have supervised either in the MSc or MBS programmes of our department. After all, they did most of the work and we learnt (and continue to do so) nearly as much from them as they from us.

In addition to these essential acknowledgements, we would like to thank the Blackhall Publishing team, especially Tony Mason, for their extreme openness to new ideas, their fast decision-making and their continued support for our projects.

Frédéric Adam and Margaret Healy
Cork, May 2000

How to Use this Book

Many books have been written and published on the topic of carrying out research and writing research reports. Some of these books are quite good and provide very good advice for researchers, either novice or advanced. The question therefore arises as to why one might want to write yet another book on doing/writing research.

The answer is very simple: as academics, we spend much of our time working with and supervising postgraduates at a variety of levels, and they keep asking the same questions all the time. Year after year, the same problems and mistakes occur, leading to the conclusion that the books that are available to our students are not totally sufficient for them to feel that they can find the answers to some of their most crucial questions.

Most texts dealing with research in the business area are more accessible to students already knowledgeable in areas of philosophy, sociology and about the multitude of 'isms' and 'ologies' that pervade the research methodology arena. However, the vast majority of courses are subject to the demands of time, and students will not have sufficient knowledge and experience of research to distil from such books exactly what it is they are looking for. We therefore decided to add our modest contribution to the collection of books already written.

This book does not set out to replace or contradict any of the work that has been done up to this point. In Part Two of this book, a bibliography of relevant publications has been included to provide signposts to further readings for students. Rather than trying to reinvent the wheel and paraphrase knowledge and explanations that have already been expertly provided by previous authors, we have attempted to provide a short cut to the essential knowledge that a student should possess when undertaking research in the context of a postgraduate degree programme. In this aspect this book differs from other books that have aimed their explanations at Ph.D. students, whose needs are largely different because of the much higher standards they must reach, or from books that have sought to describe the process of research in a general sense. We believe that postgraduate research, while it must reach significant standards, cannot and should not be expected to compare with the type of research produced by academic researchers in full flight. For this reason, we fear that many of the books currently available miss their target in terms of the help they can provide to Masters students and can even prove more misleading and disheartening as students fail to comprehend the material proposed to them.

As we see it, this book is different in the following respects:

- It is borne out of our experience with creating and administering a leading edge degree in two core disciplines in the business area, combined with several years of supervising MSc and MBS students writing major research theses.

- It concentrates on providing advice and guidelines that are well adapted to the type of research projects that Masters students, who only have limited time and resources, can be expected to undertake.

- It draws examples from a variety of business oriented research areas but concentrates on two areas of research, those of managerial accounting and management information systems, currently growing at a fast rate and which will continue to attract ever increasing numbers of students. Two particular projects, in the areas of Business Process Re-engineering and Executive Information Systems respectively, are used for illustration and example throughout the text, allowing students to see firsthand how two significant research projects progressed over time.

- Its orientation is towards more qualitative enquiries best suited to the study of modern organisations. In this respect, it may be in contrast with many other textbooks that focus on quantitative research and especially on statistically based research.

- It focuses on the essential and does not try to impose arbitrary structure or overall method on a process that is anything but structured. Rather than pretending that students' research projects must follow a number of rules, it prepares them to cope with their own personal experience with research.

- Throughout this book, the term 'dissertation' is used. However, the ideas and advice contained are relevant to all postgraduate students, regardless of whether their research requirement involves the completion of a major thesis, a minor dissertation or simply a substantial research report.

The structure of this book also deserves some explanations. It is structured in two main sections: one which focuses on the research process and another, entitled "Coping with Pandora's Box", which puts forward a number of fundamental facets of what is involved in writing dissertations, i.e. it is focused on some of those things that students need to know in order to deal with the difficulties inherent in post-graduate research activities – but which no one actually tells them about.

These two sections are different from the point of view of how they should be used. The first one is essentially sequential in its development and will be useful to all students from the start of their projects. It will help them to prepare themselves for what lies 'behind the hill', i.e. it will enable them to be prepared for the setbacks and unexpected twists and turns in their research projects. The second section contains information that may only become useful as students reach certain key stages in the research process. Thus, the sections in the second part of the book may only become useful on an ad hoc basis. We titled it "Coping with Pandora's Box" because would-be researchers can be overwhelmed by the nature and number of the problems they face when they undertake their research projects. Many pitfalls can slow down and even prematurely terminate the efforts of the most motivated students and the advice we provide in Part Two of the book may make the difference in some cases. Giving each apprentice researcher an idea of when common sense should kick in is another very important (if less tangible) aspect of what this book attempts to do through some of the sections gathered in Part Two.

Introduction:
Why Undertake Postgraduate Studies?

As we begin the 21st century, a number of pressures are changing the nature of the expectations students have when they join universities and other third level institutions. The former ideal of providing a general, high-level education as opposed to a set of skills directly applicable in a commercial environment has been questioned. In many areas, third level programmes are trying to train students so that they are able to rapidly adapt and contribute to a professional environment as opposed to just 'educating' them. At the same time, students are eager to distinguish themselves from their peers by presenting a curriculum vitae as complete, yet as original, as possible; hence the development of a wide offering of postgraduate studies.

Thus, a new style of postgraduate studies – radically different from the academically oriented, elitist style of the past - has developed and attracts increasingly large numbers of students. This is consistent with the goals pursued by educational institutions towards increasing the number of postgraduate students, as this is a reliable way to radically increase student numbers without lowering overall standards.

These pressures mean that the supervision of this new style of postgraduate students is more and more difficult. Indeed, this type of student requires far more attention than an undergraduate student, with many one on one interactions between students and lecturers. The problem is how to provide the same level of supervision when postgraduate student numbers treble or quadruple.

An equivalent dilemma faces the postgraduate student: he or she is now one of twenty, thirty or perhaps even more postgraduate students searching to give a new and unique orientation to their educational careers. Some individuals might come to have doubts in relation to the area they selected when they undertook their undergraduate studies. Other students might be late comers and might have had to settle for very general courses because their results did not enable them to register in the courses they wanted. Based on higher standards of graduate results, they are able to take postgraduate conversion courses and rejoin a more suitable career path. The benefit of a few years of relevant professional experience may enable a student to re-enter the university environment and obtain the degrees they never had the chance to study for. Whatever the reason and motivation, the postgraduate student faces what may seem to be an insurmountable obstacle to achieving his or her goals: the thesis or dissertation.

This book provides a solution for these problems. It is aimed at helping students to become more independent as they undertake research for postgraduate studies. It is aimed at constituting an alternative source of information for students and teaches them how to save time and be more efficient in the limited interaction they have with their supervisors. Thus, it will help students to understand the fundamental aspects of doing postgraduate research, not in a formal, absolute sense, but rather, with an efficient and practical approach.

Postgraduate studies in the late 1990s have enjoyed vibrant growth, and for many students this represents a fantastic opportunity to further their development. This book will become the essential travel companion and will help students get the most out of their postgraduate studies and successfully complete what should always remain an enjoyable learning experience, for both the student and supervisor alike.

PART ONE

THE RESEARCH PROCESS

In this first part, we present a breakdown in eight sections of the sequential process whereby research projects of the kind postgraduate students undertake unfold, from the first time they hear about having to do a dissertation to the time when, looking pale and haggard, they reach the Examination Office of their universities or colleges to submit their work. It is well worth mentioning at this point that the tidy sequence of tasks highlighted in research textbooks or articles on writing research does not exactly apply in this discussion. Research is messy as explained by Kaplan and Duchon (1988):

> . . . as is common in research that includes qualitative approaches, the process is messy. Impressions, interpretations, propositions and hypotheses were developed over the course of the study, a process that hardly fits the positivist ideal of objective collection of neutral or purely descriptive 'facts'. This messiness should not dismay those who experience it (p. 582).

This is an important point because it often creates much uncertainty for novice researchers who assume wrongly that their research is going off the rails as soon as they reach the stage when they no longer feel in control of their projects. At many stages in the research process, researchers may feel like their progress is being hampered by too many uncontrollable factors and that they are "going nowhere". For example, many projects are delayed by uncontrollable problems in getting interviews as target managers play "hard to catch". However frustrating such experiences may be for students, they should not lead to personal crises and must be regarded as perfectly normal incidents inherent in the research process. What truly matters is that students understand how to manage their time so that essential work can be carried out in anticipation of these idle periods in order to minimise time loss. There are many tasks that can be carried out in stages and at practically any point in the research process, such as proof reading existing chapters or preparing neat figures and tables, which can save enormous time in the final write-up stage.

Another important point that must be made is that the tidy sequential presentation of mainstream research reports is equally misleading in terms of how badly it reflects the way research takes place. In our opinions, novice researchers will find it very difficult to write a perfectly focused and relevant literature review before they have carried out at least some of the fieldwork. This does not mean that the literature reviews should not be put together before the empirical data is gathered (this would be very unwise because data collection is thus carried out from a position of ignorance and without the benefit of previous research), but it means that literature reviews may have to be fundamentally revised after the research work has been accomplished.

Similarly, few researchers have had the chance to get their research questions right before they spent some time in the organisations they wanted to investigate or before they got some of their questionnaires back through the mail. Again, it certainly does not mean that one should go out and talk to one's interviewees without the benefit of a tight framework of research questions (this just would not make any sense!), but it means that the data collected in a research project can have unanticipated strengths and weaknesses that require subtle re-framing or re-phrasing of the research questions.

Thus, research reports, while they truthfully account for the data that have been collected and the findings that can be derived from them, rarely account accurately for the process that was followed, unless this process itself was the focus of inquiry. This basic fact about research reports is not a weakness, it merely reflects the orientation of research toward the *product* rather than the *process* aspects of research projects. This bias in the reporting of research is totally acceptable and must be regarded as a convention.

The sections that follow describe a number of key stages in the research process. They have been selected because they seem to be part and parcel of most research projects. Nevertheless, they also reflect the bias of the authors of the book towards a particular type of research: qualitative and empirical research. Overall though, we feel that the presentation that follows should be applicable to most research projects. For instance, the sections dealing with the selection of a research topic will be useful to every student except perhaps for those taking part in programmes where ready-made topics are suggested. The section entitled *finding and studying existing research* will be useful to every student insofar as the review of existing research is a fundamental part of any Master thesis.

Chapter Outline: Part One – The Research Process

Chapter One opens the first part of this book and serves to present students with important aspects of postgraduate study and research that need to be considered from the outset. These include specifics regarding the timing of deadlines and deliverables, and the need to become aware of the assessment and grading arrangements governing their own particular programme. **Chapter Two** begins the dissertation in earnest, and leads students in the search for a topic. The importance of producing a good, concise research proposal and of presenting that proposal is considered. **Chapter Three** depicts the process of researching the chosen topic area and of drafting the literature review chapter(s), the research objective and research questions. Two examples are used here to guide students through the process. The typical difficulties students encounter at this stage, and how to avoid them, are dealt with.

Chapter Four beings the research methodology elements of this text in earnest. Following an introduction to the philosophical debates surrounding the nature of enquiry in general, research traditions in the social sciences, and more particularly in the areas of information systems and managerial accounting, are then considered. More specific considerations regarding research design are also considered, including: arguments for qualitative versus quantitative methods; the need for accuracy, generalisability and realism; achieving triangulation and objectivity. **Chapter Five** documents research methodologies in action, from the initial point of contact with potential sources of data through to the conclusion of data collection activities. The organisation and presentation of that research data is the subject of **Chapter Six**, whilst **Chapter Seven** deals with the production of compelling findings and the need to link those findings to previous research in the topic area, thus contributing to the process of theory building. **Chapter Eight** closes this part of the book, in dealing with the bringing together of each of the elements of the previous chapters in the production of the finished dissertation. Additional elements in the process, not sufficient to merit a complete chapter in their own right are discussed, including the Introduction, the bibliography and the appendices.

Chapter One

Finding Out What is Involved

At the start of the whole thesis/dissertation process, students would be well advised to ask a number of important questions to find out exactly what is expected of them. Theses or dissertations come in all shapes and sizes and, given how conventional the writing of research reports is, it is essential to establish from the outset the standards that will be used to judge the finished product.

Students must also make sure that they know everything there is to know about the timeframe of the dissertation. In most institutions, submission cannot take place at any time of the academic year and must comply with a number of rules for the format of the document, the number of copies and what information must appear on the front page. Students must establish these beyond reasonable doubt prior to undertaking any substantial work.

The marking scheme or assessment mechanisms must also be understood prior to investing significant efforts in one direction or another. For some degrees, the dissertation or thesis is the essential component of the marking, in which case students will be expected to do much more than they would with minor dissertations. In other degrees there might be a number of exams to sit or there might be some papers that must be produced in parallel to the thesis and which are examined separately. It is also quite frequent that the literature review, which may receive a separate mark, must be submitted at some point during the programme. The deadline for submission of the 'work in progress' documents must be understood in advance and must be incorporated into the overall schedule for completion of the thesis. In any case, students must realise that the thesis may not be the most important component in terms of marking and they must endeavour to maximise their result according to the scheme that will be applied.

While these details may sound of little interest for a student starting up on a master programme, they soon become important and it is better to avoid nasty surprises by finding out about these rules as early as possible. In relation to the timeframe, for example, a planned submission date must be set as early as possible as a target from which all other deadlines must be derived. This ultimate deadline must take into account (in reverse order):

- the time required in binding the document (especially if someone else is doing this for you[1]);

- the time necessary to print and generally produce the document, its tables and figures, its complete bibliography and appendices;

- the time required for your supervisor to review the full draft and make his or her final comments;

- a bit of spare time for contingencies, such as looking for lost references.

Altogether, these important steps may take a full three weeks and this uncompressible time must be subtracted from the deadline for submission. Thus, the target date must be known in advance and everything else stems from it.

In terms of the other 'rules', students would be well advised to enquire about any special requirements in length (in number of words, since page numbers mean little); an 'ideal' number of bibliographical references to integrate into the literature review; any rules regarding font size, margins, spacing or format (e.g. compulsory sections) or the extent of fieldwork that is expected. This last requirement can vary from programme to programme and depends on the research method selected. Typically, students can expect to be asked to carry out between ten to twenty interviews or collect 50 to 100 questionnaires. These threshold values must be negotiated with the supervisor as the study unfolds, but not too late so that additional interviews can be lined up or additional companies selected for an additional mailing (e.g. when the response rate is disappointing).

Another important point that must be established from the outset is whether research topics are going to be suggested to students or whether students are expected to find their own. Quite often, this issue is linked

---

[1] A thesis is an important document and students put considerable time and effort in producing theirs. It is therefore quite legitimate to feel proud about one's thesis and to spend a bit of money on its production. A professional binding (which must nevertheless respect the rules of presentation of your institution) will make a significant difference.

to the choice of a supervisor (or vice versa), as different members of staff have different areas of expertise and different likings. In programmes where topics are suggested, it is frequently the case that selecting one topic means selecting a supervisor. In other types of programmes, students may decide on their own topics and must then either select their supervisor from a pool of available staff or work with someone allocated to them based on the chosen topic. The principal rule in this regard is that the supervisor should be knowledgeable in the area of interest, i.e. they have recently carried out some research in it or that they are trying to develop their expertise in that area. By and large, the student must seek help in determining whether the topic they have selected is an appropriate one and this can be the beginning of a good working relationship between supervisor and supervised (the selection of a research topic is specifically addressed in Chapter 2). While students must select their topic carefully, it will always be an advantage to have an idea of what one is doing as early as possible in the course of study: much time can be spent in making up one's mind that could be spent more productively in progressing full steam ahead and refining/reframing the topic at a later stage, which is very likely to occur anyway. Few research projects actually end up looking like what the initial proposal suggested.

Chapter Two

Selecting a Research Domain – Producing a Research Proposal

The consideration of the selection of a research domain raises two fundamental questions for students embarking upon the process of research:

1. What constitutes a research topic?

2. What does a research proposal for this topic look like?

Both questions are dealt with in the sections below.

What is a Topic?

The first question is perhaps the most important, as its answer determines, at least in part, how easily students will progress along the route to the finished product. The selection of a research topic must be guided by three imperatives:

- First, and most important, students must select topics for which they feel a high degree of interest. Producing a dissertation within the timeframe of an academic year is a difficult task in itself and requires a substantial amount of effort. This may become impossible if the student's motivation fades at any point during the period.

- Second, the topic chosen must be 'researchable' in the sense that the resources required, in terms of time, equipment and finances, must not exceed those available to the student, e.g. it may not be very realistic to plan for two trips to New York to interview the director of the Wall Street Stock Exchange! Students should therefore be aware of the time and travel commitments involved in their project. Feedback from staff may indicate the need for refinement of the topic or of narrowing it down somewhat in order to make it more realistic.

- Third, the area targeted in the research project must be suitably documented by previous research. A 'good' research topic for a

Masters level thesis or dissertation can be original, but it must also be 'safe'. This means that data, bibliographical elements and existing, related research findings must be available and accessible. Thus, there is a trade-off to be resolved between the originality of the topic and its practicality from the viewpoint of the student planning to undertake the research.

Students themselves should not be the sole judge of these trade-offs and should rely largely upon the recommendations of the potential supervisors they talk to during this initial period. It is worth noting that, with a little guidance, it may not be very difficult to turn a topic initially considered too isolated from existing research or too difficult into a topic that can safely be researched. Students who are told that their topics are not suitable in this respect should seek some help from staff members of their department in order to refine their topics rather than restart from scratch.

As pointed out by Jenkins (1985),

> The most critical step in the research process is the definition
> of the research topic. This step must produce a clear and un-
> ambiguous statement of the objectives of the study. An un-
> ambiguously stated objective is essential in guiding the deci-
> sions and tradeoffs that are required in the next and subse-
> quent steps (p. 103).

Nevertheless, students should not overemphasise the importance of the choices made at the outset, as many changes can and will intervene during the course of their project.

As indicated in the following section, topics come in all shapes and forms and may be more or less well defined at the stage when students get approval for a particular research project. It is therefore not possible (nor is it particularly useful) to provide specific guidelines for writing the research proposal, notwithstanding its role as the main vehicle students use to discuss topics with potential supervisors. In essence, proposals can differ quite a lot from student to student depending upon the type of project they want to pursue, and it is impossible to say that one type of proposal is inherently better than another.

What does a Proposal Look Like?

A proposal is a written document approximately five to ten pages in length, which explains in some detail the rationale behind a research topic and provides a number of core references to support the selection of that topic. It may also give some indications of how the topic may be researched in terms of data collection and analysis, e.g. by referencing a published work that carried out similar research or by indicating the nature of the data that will be needed. In terms of how well defined the topic is at the point of writing, the preciseness of the proposal normally conditions the number of references presented and the length of the proposal. Typically, ten to twenty references can be used to support a proposal.

Even though reviewers and supervisors sometimes prefer to read proposals that specify the boundaries of research projects (i.e. what the research does and does not involve), less well defined topics may be acceptable in certain areas that are not currently well documented or that require creative thinking about data collection and analysis methods. For example, a research proposal could be very specific and involve the investigation of the application of business process re-engineering in a multi-national organisation using a case study and identifying the actual company that is going to be studied. The key informant might already have been identified and a standard literature review might be presented in summarised form.

Alternatively, a research proposal could argue that the circulation of information between the top managers of an organisation is crucial to the performance of that organisation. It could then present a number of references reporting on relevant research in the area (e.g. the work of Daft, Lengel, McLeod, Jones and their associates) and conclude that more research is required to better understand how the quality of the communication amongst the top managers of an organisation can be improved. It could suggest that focusing on a group of managers in one or several sites and interviewing a number of them would be an appropriate means of investigating the topic. Potential or definite research questions (if known) may be added in a separate section at the end.

These two topics constitute examples of opposite extremes, from one proposal where little is left to be decided upon to a proposal where much conceptual work will be required before any empirical work can realistically take place. In fact, the state or prepared-ness of the two proposals above does not reflect the amount of work put into them by the students who put them together, but rather, it reflects the difficulty of the topics proposed. The first topic is a very 'safe' topic because it contains the following elements:

- widely available literature review;

- well defined question;

- case study an obvious choice of method;

- potential organisation probably not too difficult to enter.

The second topic is much more risky in the sense that one thousand perfectly researchable questions could be derived from it. The danger is that students may never reach the stage where they actually know what they are after and get lost as a result. For such difficult topics, the difference between an average thesis and a very good thesis is often that the research questions were never tied down properly.

Ultimately, it must be understood (by both the student and the supervisor) that the research proposal is not an end in itself and does not have to reach certain cannons for presentation or content. There are exceptions to this rule insofar as some programmes include the formal marking of proposals. When the proposal constitutes a formally assessed milestone in the overall evaluation of students, it must be treated with more care and students must be careful not to lose marks by being late or doing less than is required.

Thus, the purpose of a research proposal is to support the discussion between a student and his or her potential supervisors. It enables the knowledge gained in the initial reading and discussion phase to be captured and incremented in written form. It is rarely written in one stage and is often developed after a number of iterations corresponding to the discussions that take place between the student and his or her advisers. New material is included in the proposal up to the point where enough preliminary research has been carried out and the proposal is deemed to be complete.

At this stage of the research process, students may be given the opportunity to present their projects to the staff of their department and to their peers. These presentations should be regarded as a mechanism through which important feedback can be obtained. Staff members are there to enable students to test whether chosen research designs are strong enough, thus, students should be eager to use the assessors' experience in terms of research rather than attempting to hide the weaknesses of their proposal in order to 'get away with it'. In one 'famous' session (still talked about ten years later!), a student was asked by a non-IS member of staff to define the term *information system*, but every attempt he made brought him back to the word *system* in mid-sentence. After ten minutes of unsuccessful attempts, the student finally admitted to having no precise understanding of any of the systems concepts. He was promptly provided a list of references whereby he could learn more about the theoretical framework underlying systems theory (see, for example, Checkland, 1981). Discovering such gaps in one's understanding is less damaging at an early stage than it would have been after six months (though not perhaps to one's pride!).

In such presentations, students will be expected to speak about their proposal for ten minutes, illustrating their explanations with a small number of transparencies if they so wish. They will be expected to address all aspects of their research: the process followed in selecting the topic, the rationale behind that selection, the people consulted in the initial researching of the proposal and the significant references that they are aware of. Some general guidelines on presenting materials are contained Part Two of this book.

Immediately following these presentations, assessors will provide feedback to students in the form of questions and comments that may be included in the proposals for the final submission. During this type of review, students must ensure that they clarify any issues that are unclear in relation to the topic under consideration. This includes getting exact references from assessors and, if necessary, arranging to further discuss particular aspects of the proposal at a later point. It is to the student's advantage to have as complete a proposal as possible prior to embarking upon preparation of a review of existing research.

Once it has served its purpose and the proposal has been formally accepted, the process of research can truly begin and the document as it was presented may become less relevant. Sections written on the previous research in the topic area may subsequently be inserted into the literature review chapter(s), but this is not the main purpose of the proposal. The proposal will still be used as a reference document in the subsequent stages of the research and may be of use in obtaining access to potential research sites and convincing potential informants to take part in the research, but it is unlikely that the finished thesis or dissertation will have respected all aspects of the proposal (if any). This must not be regarded as a weakness of the process that was followed, but merely as an illustration of the tortuous nature of the research process itself.

Chapter Three

Finding and Studying Existing Research

Importance of the Literature Review

This stage of the research process is a very important one. Of course, it can be argued that all stages are important, but in the context of postgraduate research it is particularly essential to present a strong review of the literature in that much of the final assessment of the work will focus on this section of the dissertation. Master students are not expected to produce ground shattering, totally novel research that produces exceptional new findings, but a convincing, well structured review of relevant research is expected. Like other aspects of postgraduate research, this may appear to be conventional, but one of the purposes of Masters dissertations is to demonstrate the additional understanding and knowledge gained by students in a particular domain and to show their ability to synthesise and organise the material selected within the context of a well defined research project. This purpose is specifically served by the literature review. Thus, a good, solid and well focused literature review is essential in writing a high calibre dissertation, whatever the level at which it is presented.

Four functions of any literature review have been put forward by Marshall and Rossman (1989), which provides a useful means of structuring this chapter of the book. The literature review serves to:

- demonstrate the underlying assumptions behind the research topic;

- show that the researcher is knowledgeable about the related research and research traditions in the subject area;

- help in identifying gaps in the previous research within which the proposed study can be placed;

- aid in refining and redefining the research questions towards placing them within the context of the research tradition in the subject area.

The literature review constitutes the theoretical foundation of the research and outlines the boundaries of the research domain considered. It must present in a coherent chapter (or a series of two or three chapters) the research results that justify the focus on the research topic and those that are going to be used in designing the study, both from a conceptual and from a methodological point of view. Ultimately, it must present in its conclusions a concise statement of the research objective and an outline of the research questions that are being pursued in the research project.

Occasionally, the concept of literature review can also be assigned a broader meaning to include an additional chapter or section dealing specifically with the methodological issues relevant to the research. This is usually the case where the research methodologies previously employed in the subject area have had a fundamental impact upon the data gathering and subsequent theoretical development and model-building in that area. By research methodology we mean the formalisation of the research framework and the set of methods that will be applied by the researcher. This normally involves fairly standard descriptions of available methods and sometimes a short discussion about the different paradigms that have been adopted by researchers in the history of science.

At higher levels, such as that of Ph.D. candidates, this section of the thesis is required to display some evidence of a more personal understanding of the issues involved in the adherence to a particular paradigmatic position. At Master level, candidates can rely on more simplistic presentations that focus on the aims of the research and the specific methods used to achieve these. This being said, candidates are always well advised to seek clarification from their supervisors/course directors as to how thorough they are expected to be in relation to the whole methodological debate.[1] In this book we take the approach that the methodological debate is an important one, which is a linked but separate issue to the construction of the literature review. It is dealt with in Chapters 4 and 5.

The third function of the literature review is to help identify

---

[1] It is the experience of the authors that the debate around research methods/paradigms is very cultural and subject-dependent. Thus, in France, students are rarely expected to worry about methodologies, whereas UK candidates must spend more time understanding the different paradigms available to them.

how the proposed study fits within the context of previous research. This will have been partially established as a research need in the proposal document (dealt with in Chapter 2) and the aim of the literature review is to consolidate that need – formally described as the 'research objective' – within existing academic writings and research work.

Finally, once the overall research objective has been stated and in a sense justified within the domains of existing research, individual research questions are formulated, refined and redefined towards answering that research objective.

Sourcing Material

One of the characteristics of doing postgraduate research at the dawn of the third millennium is that the amount of information available has increased considerably. This unprecedented increase in the volume of material around us is compounded by the fact that libraries, traditional sources of research data, can only acquire a small portion of what is published either electronically or on paper. Essentially, the problem of access to information has become an interface problem whereby the conceptual search (in the mind) has been replaced by a practical search for the *killer* references amongst the countless different sources available.

Thus, the nature of the literature review stage of postgraduate research has changed dramatically over the last few years and it has never been so important to try to ensure that one has the most up to date references. In a way, this is regrettable because this increase in volume often militates against the use of older material, much of which is quite interesting and valuable. Many indexes and search engines available on the Internet begin in 1990, which only skims the surface of previous research in many areas. Even in the 'recent' disciplines, such as management, it would be a mistake to ignore the earlier work of Fayol (1916), Carlson (1951), Steward (1967), Simon (1957, 1977) or Mintzberg (1973). It is indeed a characteristic of the social sciences that more recent work rarely invalidates previous research to the extent that nothing could be learnt from it. As noted by March and Simon (1993) in the second edition of their landmark book Organisations (in reference to the first edition from 1958),

> we still enjoy reading the book from time to time and are surprised more often by the things that we knew then, but have forgotten, than by the things that we know now, but did not know then (p. 1).

Students would therefore be well advised to remember that new does not mean beautiful and old does not mean useless. It is best advised to try to find a balance between newer and more glamorous material and older, more traditional material in order to demonstrate some depth of reading. By and large, these two types of material must be obtained using different sources and ways of collection. The former (newer) material can be sourced on the Internet (see Part Two) or through the use of a CD-ROM search in the local library, while the latter (older) material must be identified from discussions with supervisors and second-hand referencing in other articles from high standing researchers.

What does a Literature Review Look Like?

Students may initially be puzzled and feel rather unsure about what they are really expected to produce. Unfortunately, it is not possible to provide strict guidelines for structuring literature reviews simply because the structure should emerge from the contents of the topic researched. Thus, a contingency approach can be suggested whereby a careful examination of available material – especially journal articles – provides some clues to a potential structure for the literature review. The same method can actually be suggested as a means to get ideas regarding the methods to apply to a particular research topic. Thus, studying examples of previous research projects can be a useful source of knowledge. In every department in every university in the world, course directors and supervisors proudly display the dissertations and theses that have been submitted down through the years. These constitute a good starting point for students who are uncertain what a suitable topic or a good literature review looks like and can also be used as a focused source of references. Naturally, it is not acceptable to attempt to replicate a study that has already been carried out by someone else and to hope that no one in the staff will remember (this is highly unlikely anyway). At the same time, good ideas can emerge from a quick look around the archives of your own masters programmes; MBS and MSc students regularly raid our shelves.

However, in order to write a good literature review it is important to understand a bit more about the process that one will typically follow when writing such a document.

Students will typically write their literature reviews at a time when they are not yet totally sure what their topics are.[2] In many cases, their proposal may be the first draft of the literature review – a draft that still requires a lot of work! Using this initial blueprint as a framework, students obtain additional references that they think are relevant and try to integrate them into their live document so that it is incremented slowly but surely and gets progressively closer to the finished product. The consequence of this process is that the first full draft of a literature review is often very rough in a number of ways, as highlighted below:

- The structure may be lacking in clarity and purpose: as students increment material in a semi-random manner (as they discover new references they like), they wonder where they should insert the new material and are tempted to create new sections every time a new article or book seems to be saying something different, instead of analysing the roots of the debates they have identified and making an argument. This is acceptable initially, but must be corrected when the amount of material collected is deemed sufficient by the supervisor.

- The balance between the different sections may be wrong: some of the references obtained may be quite specific and present detailed results of experiments that have been carried out. Students are tempted to report extensively on these very tangible results whereas other, more tenuous or less well researched areas only get a few lines even though they are just as important from the point of view of the research. This must be corrected either by cutting back the sections that are overly detailed or by finding additional references to cover the weaker areas.

- There might still be a number of gaps in the analysis presented: this happens because the topic was not totally defined at the

---

[2] It has appeared in discussions with colleagues in other departments, that some supervisors feel happier when students have a reasonably definitive understanding of what they are after. Students must follow their supervisor's advice in this respect.

start of the writing phase. Areas that did not seem important must now be included because they feature prominently in the research questions. These shifts in the research topic are largely unavoidable and are good news in the sense that they indicate the student's increasing familiarity with his or her topic. They may occur at different stages in the research process (and unfortunately sometimes quite near the end as the empirical data is being analysed and the thesis must be reframed somewhat). This is not a problem per say, but the additional efforts required in aligning the literature review with the overall thesis must be done because such lack of harmony is precisely what differentiates the bad from the good thesis.

- The emphasis may be wrong: this equally frequent problem occurs for the same reasons highlighted in the previous paragraph and must also be corrected by rewriting key sections, such as the general introduction and conclusion, and key connecting paragraphs that explain the linkages between the main blocks and describe what is done in the different sections of the literature review.

A number of practical guidelines are offered at the end of this chapter as to how to go about the process of constructing a literature review, and are illustrated using two examples of actual postgraduate research projects. This should be of use to students as a means of overcoming the difficulties mentioned above, but the most important problems that typically linger in literature reviews at that first draft stage reside in the style that is used by students and in the weakness of the argumentation. These two problems are critical and are treated separately in the next paragraphs.

Students sometimes find it difficult to adapt to the style that is required for thesis/dissertation writing. It is quite important that they understand what is suitable early on, otherwise they face tricky and time-consuming rewriting exercises that can be disheartening to say the least. The first step in acquiring the proper style is to carefully avoid using personal pronouns, possessive adjectives or possessive pronouns in the first or second person (either singular or plural). Thus, I, we, us, our, etc. are all forbidden and must be replaced by neutral statements. Beyond this rather trivial requirement, students must ensure that they stick to what has been researched and documented before and avoid making general state-ments such as 'it is obvious that...' when their personal opinion is the only basis for saying so. As such, common sense is not suffi-cient for including an argument or an idea in a literature review (see also the discussion about research methodologies in the next section of this book). Thus, students will have to rely on the refer-ences they have found in order to build up their argumentation.

However, they must also be careful not to fall at the second hurdle, i.e. not to merely string together short paragraphs present-ing the results of different studies without 'doing anything' with them. This results in poor literature reviews that fail to analyse the research they describe and, more importantly, fail to demonstrate its validity and relevance to the research project. A good literature review is not a catalogue of previous research; it must add value to the simple presentation of a selection of existing work.

A literature review must also be a synthesis of the work pre-sented which gives the reader the benefit of not having to replicate the research work carried out by the student. For example, a thesis which attempts to apply the literature on critical success factors to the analysis of an organisation's competitive advantage must seek to present a framework that can be readily used by other research-ers for the purpose of similar research projects they wish to under-take. This added value and contribution to existing debates can sometimes be done by way of rich diagrams integrating earlier con-tributions whose complementary nature is therefore highlighted and showing how a broad segment of previous research fits together. An example of such a diagram is shown in Figure 3.1. This figure was presented by a student researching the role and contribution of information systems (IS) staff in organisations and how to enable them to develop ISs that truly support the strategy of their organi-sation. The key elements of the research framework have been brought together on the diagram and the key linkages between them are explained by reference to a number of articles or books that provide specific findings relevant to these elements. Thus, this model is supported by thirteen references, which gives it greater validity and credibility. The idea that rich displays are a very at-tractive and efficient vehicle for integrating literature and present-ing data and conclusions is further examined in chapters 6 and 7.

Figure 3.1: Integrating previous research into a rich framework

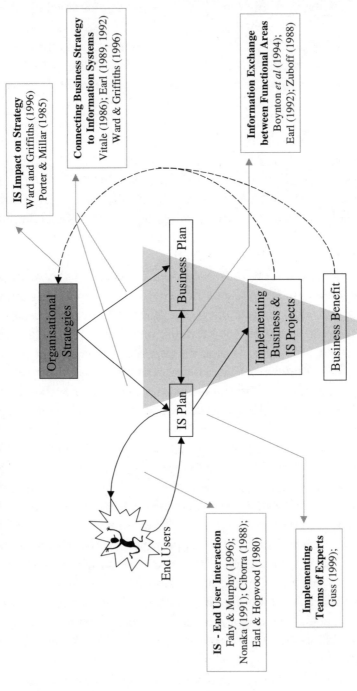

IS Impact on Strategy
Ward and Griffiths (1996)
Porter & Millar (1985)

**Connecting Business Strategy
to Information Systems**
Vitale (1986); Earl (1989, 1992)
Ward & Griffiths (1996)

**Information Exchange
between Functional Areas**
Boynton *et al* (1994);
Earl (1992); Zuboff (1988)

Organisational
Strategies

Business Plan

Implementing
Business &
IS Projects

Business Benefit

IS Plan

End Users

IS - End User Interaction
Fahy & Murphy (1996);
Nonaka (1991); Ciborra (1988);
Earl & Hopwood (1980)

**Implementing
Teams of Experts**
Guss (1999);

Adapted from Deasy (1999)

Finally, in its conclusions the literature review must present a definitive statement of the research objective and an outline of the research questions which is detailed enough to be used as a guide in the rest of the research project. The operationalisation, i.e. the selection of the research methods to be used by the researcher in order to gather the empirical data required in answering the questions, and the methodological framework used to analyse that data can be left for later chapters dealing with methodological issues. However, the literature review must funnel the previous research examined by the researcher into a clear statement of the research objectives (as in Jenkins, 1985).

The Literature Review: Some Practical Guidelines

Writing a literature review is not always an easy process and it may take a while to shape up through a series of iterations which reflect the increasing degree of understanding that each student has of his or her own rcscarch topic. As we were once told by a respected professor at University College Cork, "You can write an average dissertation without having a precise idea of what you are at...but it sure helps a lot when you find out!"

Given the individual nature of the endeavour, exact structures for writing the literature review element of a research project cannot really be put forward to students. However, there are certain prerequisites and skills which must be demonstrated, in particular those of endurance, the ability to read large amounts of material and the ability to structure and synthesise large amounts of material into a coherent and in-depth review. Two examples are used throughout this section to illustrate the points made in the preceding discussion and to allow students to experience the process of a literature review development in a more active sense than if simply provided with an unillustrated checklist.[3]

---

[3] Note that the examples used in this section are intended as examples of the process of compiling the literature review, and are not intended to be reflective of the current state of research in the respective subject areas. Indeed, given that both are taken from actual research dissertations concluded in the early and mid 1990s, it is most likely that research in those areas will have moved forward somewhat.

1. Identify the general area you propose to study and briefly consider why it is important to carry out research in that area. This
   set of statements will ultimately form the introductory section
   of the chapter, but for the moment will simply serve to com-
   mence the literature review process (See Examples 1a and 1b).

Example 1a: Business Process Re-engineering[4]

*In the 1990s there has been a growing awareness of and need for
strategic orientation and competitive focusing of businesses,
whereby organisations are constantly seeking to change and evolve
to make best use of the opportunities offered by the technologies
of the 21st century. The awareness of the need for change has led
to a search for the means to bring it about. Business process re-
engineering (BPR) has been advanced as a means of achieving
the innovative, fundamental change deemed necessary to ensure
long-term survival and prosperity. However, little empirical research exists on the topic.*

Example 1b: Executive Information Systems[5]

*In comparison to the improvements they brought to production
activities and administrative tasks, computers have done relatively
little to support the work of top managers. Executive information
systems (EIS) are intended to change the vision executives have
of computer systems and are designed to meet their information
needs and to support the type of tasks that they have to perform.
Not enough is known, however, about the information flows used
by top executives in their work and this relative ignorance pre-
vents the effective development of the concept of an information
system for executives.*

---

[4] Healy, M. (1995), *An Empirical Investigation of Business Process Re-engineering as a Mechanism for Change*, Unpublished MBS dissertation, National University of Ireland.
[5] Adam, F (1992), *The Identification and Analysis of Information Flows among Senior Executives – An Empirical Study*, Unpublished MBS dissertation, National University of Ireland.

2. Define any titles or phrases used that may be subject to misinterpretation by the reader or whose exact definition as used in the research study is fundamental to your line of argument (and may perhaps be different to those used by other researchers in the subject). Your supervisor is your best guide on this point. For instance, in Example 1b above, clarification should be given of the different terms used throughout the 1980s in the IS domain, e.g. EIS, ESS, MIS, DSS, etc. (see, for example, Rockart and Van Bullen, 1985; Gulden and Ewers, 1989).

3. Consider the main building blocks of your argument. Your proposal will have already alluded to, if not explicitly stated, the 'research gap'; the literature review presents a justification as to that gap's existence. However, you cannot just 'jump in'. The task is to present the various facets of the debate and in the process build up the platform upon which your own work, your chosen research methodology and data collection tools and ultimately your contribution to the theory-building process can and must be defended. This includes stating any significant areas within the research topic that are outside the scope of your research project (See Examples 2a and 2b).

Example 2a: Business Process Re-engineering

- Introduce the idea of innovative change.
- Business Process Re-engineering as a concept for such innovative change.
  - Definition of BPR.
  - Elements of a re-engineering strategy.
- Is Business Process Re-engineering simply a Marketing Myth?
  - The effect of change initiatives on employees.
  - Is BPR simply an another of the consultants' tools?
- The Re-engineering Team
  - Various team members and roles.

- Information requirements of BPR.
- The Role of the Accountant and of Management Accounting.
- A Contribution to the Literature.

Example 2b: Executive Information Systems

- The Changing Organisational Environment Facing Top Executives.
  - The growing importance of information.
  - Increased complexity of the environment.
- The Role of the Top Executive.
  - The different nature of managerial work.
  - The activities of executives re: problem solving and decision-making.
  - The activities of executives re: strategy formulation.
- The Nature of Information.
  - Definition of information.
  - The message as the vehicle of information: form/ medium/etc.
- Computer-based Information Systems.
  - Evolution of computer-based information systems.
  - Development of EIS systems.
- Matching the potential contribution of Computer Systems with the role of top executives.

---

4. Build the 'roadmap' of your literature review around these building blocks and see if you can argue your way into and out of successive headings. You will save much time and energy (not to mention subsequent redrafts and soul-searching) if you can agree on the suitability of this outline with your supervisor. The end product, as you will see in the examples continued below, is a set of headings (the roadmap) which must be fleshed out and suitably referenced. Essentially, these headings form a table of contents for the chapter(s) and demonstrate the progression of your arguments in a clear and purposeful manner. It will become readily apparent to both you and your supervisor if the arguments are unbalanced or you are omitting any major areas of literature (either accidentally or otherwise). This step is illustrated in Examples 3a and 3b.

Example 3a: Business Process Re-engineering

1.0 INTRODUCTION

1.1 A PARADIGM FOR CHANGE AND INNOVATION: Organisations, in order to survive and grow, need to be constantly aware of their position and that of their competitors in the environment facing the industry and the economy in general. Opportunities as well as threats pose the need for major change, but the desire for change is not always matched by an awareness of how to bring it about. BPR has been proposed as a management paradigm of the 1990s to enable fundamental organisational change and facilitate in managing a dynamic, global working environment rather than simply replicating or automating pieces of physical work. The literature, in informing of the benefits and gains to be made from and through BPR, has, however, created a two-fold effect: BPR has been established as a concept for innovative change, but so too has BPR, the marketing myth. Each of these is discussed under the following sub-headings.

1.2 BPR: A CONCEPT FOR INNOVATIVE CHANGE: This section draws on existing literature on BPR and sets out the characteristics and guiding principles that distinguish BPR as a means of change creation and management.

1.2.1 Business Process Re-engineering – An introduction: This gives a definition of re-engineering, based on existing literature.

1.2.2 A Framework for BPR: Different authors have proposed various re-engineering frameworks, and they are each considered here, both individually and in relation to each other. Various enablers and drivers of BPR are also identified and discussed. Four defining facets of re-engineering are identified for more in-depth discussion as per sections 1.2.3-1.2.6.

1.2.3 Process Approach: Use of the value chain in the organisation to identify the core and secondary processes.

1.2.4 Benchmarking towards a customer focus: Definition of benchmarking; benchmarking helps define and focus the vision of the re-engineered process, and can add a sense of urgency by placing previously accepted organisational process performance levels into the wider context of a global competitive environment. Two reasons for the importance of the customer focus are the segregation of the mass market into several segments, some even as small as a single customer, and the threat of backward integration lending power to the consumer over the producer.

1.2.5 Innovative and Fundamental Change: BPR proposes innovative rather than incremental change, so previously assumed organisational tenets must be questioned - management and functional hierarchies, costs, cycle times. Redesign of work necessitates performance measures, controls and management reward systems must be redesigned to emphasise process goals and team work, otherwise it is "merely rearranging the deckchairs on the Titanic" (Hammer and Champy, 1993, p.107).

1.2.6 Use of Information Technology: IT possibly represents the key enabler in BPR projects; however, it can also act as a constraint given existing organisational legacies of hardware and software; need to integrate technology with people, processes and tasks.

1.3 BPR – THE MARKETING MYTH: Much literature also exists positing BPR as a marketing-driven package created by consultants (?), without much underlying substance or validity, to fill the gap left by previously unsuccessful approaches to organisational change. Links to previous tools, techniques and change methods; effects on the workforce; abuse of the opportunities offered via IT; lack of independently validated examples of successful BPR applications running from initiation to implementation and subsequent assessment; multi-disciplinary nature of BPR.

1.4 ROLES WITHIN THE RE-ENGINEERING TEAM: Re-engineering requires cross-functional co-operation within an organisation, in particular given the aspects described in Section 1.2. The discipline of managerial accounting is well placed to meet the information provision and analysis phases of such projects.

1.4.1 The Re-engineering Team: The roles to be filled within the re-engineering exercise as put forward in the literature are examined; the importance of the 'team'.

1.4.2 The Accountancy Function: Accountancy and management accountancy in particular offers huge potential in meeting the informational and analysis needs of an organisation involved in re-engineering. Involvement in such projects answers the stated need to broaden the focus of the discipline as expressed in the growing body of literature appearing under the umbrella of Strategic Management Accounting in both professional and academic publications.

1.5 CONTRIBUTION TO THE LITERATURE: Lack of empirical research makes BPR a high-risk strategy. Existing literature is predominantly normative, with little consideration of the extent to which functional 'experts' are enablers of or barriers to such change mechanisms. Development of a concise research objective.

In the next example, the researcher has chosen to organise the literature into two separate chapters. This is a sensible approach in contexts where the field of research is very broad and cannot be sensibly funnelled down to a statement of the research objective across three or four main building blocks, or when two radically different areas of research are drawn upon, i.e. EIS and management. The first chapter concentrates on the nature of managerial work and the managerial tasks that could benefit from the support of computer systems. The second chapter is concerned with analysing previous investigations in the area of computer systems for top management as well as the examples of such systems that are currently available (See Example 3b).

Example 3b: Executive Information Systems

CHAPTER ONE: EXECUTIVES AND THEIR INFORMATION FLOWS

1.0 INTRODUCTION: Given the increased information intensity in the working environment of modern society, there is a need for timely, accurate and efficient information systems within organisations. Explanation of the structure of the chapter.

1.1 THE EVOLUTION OF SOCIETY: Ideas have been put forward to explain the emergence of this new society (the post-industrial society) characterised by increasing competition, growing value of information and the increasing importance of an efficient transmission of information.

1.1.1 The New Characteristics: The growing importance of knowledge and technology.

1.1.2 The Necessary Adaptations: Contingency theories whereby organisations survive by adapting to fit with their changing environments raise the need to consider the growing importance of having an efficient circulation of information within the organisation.

1.1.3 The New Value of Information: The perception of information itself is changing within organisations; emergence of a more strategic role linked to the organisation's value chain and to concepts of competitive advantage.

1.2 THE TRANSMISSION OF INFORMATION: In considering how to efficiently handle the information flows of executives, it is critical to identify exactly what constitutes information and how it is processed in organisations.

1.2.1 What is Information – A Working Definition: Various definitions of information: a corporate resource; an ability to 'make sense' of a given situation; processed data.

1.2.2 The Message – Vehicle of Information: Communication of information is performed via messages; thus it is important to consider what messages consist of:

1.2.2.1 *The Form of the Signal:* Meaning is communicated via 'hard' and 'soft' data, and in verbal and written form.

1.2.2.2*The Communication Media:* Considering the richness of the communication medium in relation to the form of the signal towards reducing uncertainty and reducing equivocality. Daft and Lengel Framework, 1984; Jones, Saunders and McLeod Framework, 1988.

1.2.2.3*The Source of Information:* Varying importance of various sources of information used by executives, e.g. direct verbal contact; documents; presence at events, etc.

1.2.3 Information in the Environment: The decision-making process of executives is also linked to events occurring outside the organisation.

1.3 HOW INFORMATION RELATES TO THE EXECU-TIVES' ROLES: A study of the information flows surrounding executives demands the complement of a study of the tasks that required the information in the first place. This sub-section considers the role(s) of executives within organisations.

1.3.1 The Nature of Managerial Work: An overview of the principal findings of both theoretical and empirical research concerned with learning more about the way managers actually work, what difficulties they face and how to train would-be managers in a more efficient manner.

1.3.1.1*A Brief History of Management as a Science*: Starting with Anthony, 1965: three levels of managerial tasks – strategic planning, management control and operation control – each having different information requirements. Gorry and Scott Morton Framework, 1971.

1.3.1.2*The Findings of the Field Studies*: Carlson, 1951; Steward, 1967; Mintzberg, 1973; formulation of interpersonal roles, informational roles and decisional roles of top executives; the manager as an information processing system. Monitoring, storing and disseminating information are three essential elements of the role(s) of executives which are considered further in Sect 1.3.2-1.3.4 below.

1.3.2 The Activities of Detection: Information flow and media used in identifying problems and opportunities facing the organisation, and formulated into organisational strategy (Pounds, 1969).

1.3.3 Decision-Making Processes: Some key lessons are to be learnt from previous studies of managerial decision-making, for example, Mintzberg *et al.*, 1976; Hickson *et al.*, 1985; Eisenhardt, 1989, 1990.

1.3.4 The Activities of Communication: Tendency for information flows to be attached to the 'person' rather than the 'function'; need for balance between hard and soft information; failures in organisational communication flows.

1.3.5 The Activities of Strategy Elaboration: Much of the executive's role concerns strategy formation Need to consider the information flows involved.

1.3.5.1 *Definition:* Definition of strategy.

1.3.5.2 *Management Control Systems and Strategy*: How information is relevant to the elaboration and the control of the organisational strategy circulated in the organisation; the management control system as the means through which the achievement of organisational objectives is monitored; the adequacy of accounting information. Mintzberg, 1978, 1985 – the "grass-roots" model of strategy formation.

1.4   CONCLUSION: Summary of the previous sub-sections.

CHAPTER TWO: AN INFORMATION SYSTEM FOR EXECUTIVES

2.0   INTRODUCTION: Since the 1960s, designers of systems have been trying to create applications that would serve the information needs of executives. The concept of computer-based information systems and in particular the more recent developments aimed specifically at the information needs of executives are considered. The use of electronic capabilities to facilitate managerial activities in organisations is evaluated in terms of their potential to serve the information flow needs of such activities. Structure of the Chapter is explained.

2.1   AN INTRODUCTION TO COMPUTER-BASED INFORMATION SYSTEMS

2.1.1 Different Types of Systems ...: Different eras of development characterised by different emphases have produced different types of information systems, including management information systems; decision support systems; office automation systems; transaction processing systems.

2.1.2 ...for Different Types of Applications: Links these different types of systems back to the activities and information needs of executives dealt with in the previous chapter of the Literature Review.

2.2 FOR OR AGAINST A COMPUTER-BASED INFORMA-TION SYSTEM FOR EXECUTIVES

2.2.1 The EIS Connection: Executive information systems represent the latest technological offering in computer-based information systems and have been selected for evaluation within the framework of this study, given its particular focus on the information flows of executives. This section defines EIS and considers the differences between EIS and earlier systems and systems applications considered in Sections 2.1.1 and 2.1.2.

2.2.2 Anything New?: Benefits from EIS.

2.2.3 Some Examples of EIS: British Airways story as one of the earliest EIS; other examples to be found in the literature.

2.2.4 Surveys of the Field: Research evidence on the documented roles and uses of EIS; implications re: the information flows of executives.

2.2.5 A Real Definition of EIS?: Development of a suitable definition of EIS, that definition to be constructed from the key features and capabilities of such systems as found from the review of literature and previous research.

2.3 THE CONTRIBUTION OF ELECTRONIC CAPABILI-TIES TO MANAGERIAL ACTIVITIES: Consideration of the functions of EIS that contribute to the work of executives as discussed in the previous review chapter.

2.3.1 Access to Current Status and 'Drill down' Facilities: The ability of EIS to access large amounts of data, enhance the short-term planning and control systems of managers and access external (environment-related) information.

2.3.2 EIS as a Communication Tool: How can EIS help solve organisational communication difficulties regarding the length of the communications chain and deal with issues of information overload, delay and distortion; two relevant applications are discussed in Sections 2.3.2.1 and 2.3.2.2.

2.3.2.1 *Group Decision Support Systems:* Can these improve the decisions made by managers?

2.3.2.2 *Electronic Messaging Systems:* Potential of e-mail as a viable, cost-effective medium of communication; potential problems re: information overload, junk mail, degree of formality, etc.

2.3.3 EIS and the Executives' Mental Models: Integration of the discussion in this chapter with that presented in chapter one.

2.4 CONCLUSION: Top executives are still not convinced about the usefulness of technology. The potential in terms of communication of electronic systems has been demonstrated, but such systems are not specific enough in their use and their capabilities to fit exactly the needs of executives. Development of a specific research objective and exact research questions.

5. A few points regarding your research road map:

- The number of levels under which you create sub-headings is entirely dependent upon the level of detail and stream of thought being followed in that particular section. There is no right or wrong number; the objective is simply to structure the argument into sensible divisions. The absolute maximum, however, should be four levels of detail – if you need more than that, then either the contents of each sub-heading are insufficient to merit being dealt with separately or the contents are of such importance that, rather than one sub-heading to four-plus levels of detail, you really need to create sub-headings at a higher level.

- One cannot put an absolute number on the amount of references required under each heading and sub-section, even though particular supervisors may require a prespecified minimum quantity. You are aiming to produce a comprehensive and balanced picture of the literature and previous research in the subject area, and that should be your guide. Include the references you have already collected under the relevant sections of your road map and that should give you an initial idea of how much more research you need to do. More information on sourcing relevant literature is contained in the Part Two of this book.

- A particular piece of research may be relevant to more than one area of the literature review. That is not a problem! Indeed, most research projects tend to hinge on a core or central article, book or document. Beware, however, that you do not over-rely on one or two sources.

- The 'introduction' section is the last piece of the chapter you will write. These paragraphs serve to guide the reader through the document and to point him or her in the direction of your argument. Thus, you will find it easiest to write once you have already determined, on paper, what that argument is.

6. Start writing! Once you have your road map drafted and agreed with your supervisor, you have no excuse! The search for relevant literature is an ongoing endeavour throughout the research project. Once you have accumulated enough materials to build the road map, you have enough to begin writing. The road map is not cast in stone and you may want to change elements of it later, for example, when you have completed data collection activities. On a practical note: you would be well advised to format your growing document from the start as per the submission requirements of your university. By this it is meant using the correct font size; left, right, top and bottom of page margins; correct line spacing, etc. This will save much editing time in later periods when you are putting your completed dissertation together (see also: Practical Publishing in Part Two).

7. The development of the research objective and associated research questions represents the final hurdle in the literature review process. It is a matter of individual and supervisor choice as to where exactly within the final dissertation document you will present these items to the reader - many students have chosen to do so within the opening pages of the research methodology chapter rather than at the end of the literature review chapter. The process of outlining or building the research objective and questions, however, properly occurs at the end of the literature review phase.

A research objective forms the ultimate conclusion of the literature-based debate you have presented, and it must be justified, through the previously presented argument and discussion, as being that whose achievement will add to knowledge in the subject area. Essentially, you are stating in one sentence the aim of your research project. (You may find this objective is useful at a later date also in drafting the title page of your dissertation).

Answering the research objective is operationalised via a number of mutually exclusive research questions, the answers to which, when analysed, will provide for the successful attainment of that objective. Perhaps the best way to understand this is to consider the two examples used earlier (See Examples 4a and 4b).

Example 4a: Business Process Re-engineering

Summary of the Literature Review

The dynamic environment and increasingly competitive nature of both domestic and international competition facing industry has led to a growing awareness of and need for strategic orientation and competitive focus. Organisations are caught between the conflicting demands and benefits of existing mass-manufacturing technology, thought and techniques and the increasing need to be responsive to customer needs while adapting to changing economic conditions. Business process re-engineering (BPR) has been advanced as a strategy towards achieving the innovative, fundamental change deemed necessary in many organisations to ensure long-term economic survival and prosperity.

Proponents of re-engineering claim that unlike previous concepts, e.g. total quality management, which served to bring about incremental change, BPR, when properly applied and managed, generates fundamental, radical and lasting change. Drawing from existing literature on the BPR concept, the characteristics and guiding principles identified as distinguishing BPR as a valid means of change management have been set out in this chapter. These include an emphasis on process rather then product; the radical, fundamental rethinking of organisational activities; an absence of functional hierarchies; and an outward-looking emphasis on customer satisfaction.

The arguments for BPR being a myth perpetuated for marketing purposes without much underlying substance and validity were also examined. The lack of a common definition, techniques and characteristics across reported instances of re-engineering, as well as the previous existence of many of its underlying elements, are cited by various authors as reasons justifying its dismissal as a new and different means of change management.

More recent literature on BPR is recognising the importance of human factors in re-engineering initiatives, with the implementation phase suggested as being the most likely point of failure for many projects. Information technology and human and organisational factors are posited as key enablers; competitive pressure, customer orientation, finance, the need for better co-ordination and management of functional interdependencies and the impact of a changing business culture are seen as the main drivers of re-engineering change. A variety of views are presented on who should be involved in a BPR project highlighting, above all else, the need for efficient and effective team management.

The true potential of the re-engineering team seems to lie in its ability to integrate across structural and functional boundaries and to redesign and energise the core processes of an organisation. Given the critical nature of the organisational requirements of this endeavour in that they are multi-faceted, cross functional and of both quantitative and qualitative format, management accounting, both in terms of the discipline and of its participants, would seem to be ideally situated to play a key role in such teams.

Research Gap

Existing literature on BPR is predominantly normative in nature, with a paucity of empirically based, descriptive research documenting BPR change initiatives from original inception through to ultimate implementation, measurement and review. BPR as a concept for innovative change needs to be examined to determine if its various elements as defined and documented in the literature are evidenced in practice. By its nature, BPR is a high-risk strategy for change, affecting more than just the operational activity of an organisation. Thus, it is important to determine how re-engineering as a change mechanism should be managed within organisations, and the extent to which " 'experts' in various functional fields are barriers to, or facilitators of change" (Coulson-Thomas, 1994, p. 111). Of particular interest to the researcher is the issue of management accountancy involvement in BPR: are management accountants adopting a proactive or reactive approach to re-engineering?

Research Objective and Research Questions

The research gap centres around the lack of descriptive research on re-engineering, and has been formulated into the following research objective:

"To provide, based on empirical evidence, a detailed description of business process re-engineering as a mechanism for change, with particular reference to the role of management accountancy as an area of functional expertise."

The description the researcher provides must, however, be 'bound' or constructed in some way so as to enable data collection, data analysis and theory development activities to proceed. Thus, a number of research questions were developed:

1. Does BPR represent a concept for innovative change?

2. What are the barriers to and enablers of successful BPR?

3. What is the extent of the role of management accountancy in BPR?

Example 4b: Executive Information Systems

Summary of the Literature Review

The area of executive information systems or, in general, of information systems for top managers has been a plentiful area of research over the last 25 years. Much research has been carried out which was concerned with the development of systems that top managers can use to improve their effectiveness and efficiency in relation to a number of key elements of their role, such as decision-making, problem finding or leadership. This dissertation concerns the study of the information flows amongst top managers in order to establish in what specific ways a computer system could support the exchanges of information and the communication of executives.

The evolution of modern organisations has meant that information and its efficient circulation amongst organisational actors have become increasingly important. Existing research on the role of information in management was considered. The researcher then proposed a definition for information and analysed research available about the main vehicle for information: messages. The chapter then went on to explain how information relates to the work of executives and focused on each of the major types of activities that are normally as-

sociated with management: detection (problems and opportunities), communication, strategy elaboration, decision-making, etc.

Three main factors were found to be important for the research project: (1) the territory on which technological solutions were going to be applied had to be well understood; (2) the information flows supporting the main activities of managers had to be identified accurately; and (3) issues that had been documented as real causes of concern to executives in relation to their usage of and reliance on information systems needed to be documented.

The second chapter looked at the different types of systems that have been identified in previous research and their applications, in particular the concept of EIS. There are some fundamental disagreements between authors in the field, thus, the researcher puts forward a more robust definition for EIS that could be used for the purpose of the research project, leading to a classification of the major functionalities that have been provided to organisational actors using computer systems.

Gaps in the Literature

More information needs to be collected on the nature of information usage by top managers so as to obtain living examples of executives' information networks (as in Kotter, 1984 and in Mintzberg, 1973). The activities of 'detection', 'decision-making' and 'control' of managers need to be better understood as they relate to information and the information flows of managers in order to assess the potential of computer systems in supporting these activities. The value adding effect of managers' handling of the information they collect needs to be analysed for the same reasons. The opinions of executives regarding the computer systems they used and of information systems in general have to be assessed so as to ascertain that the support of top managers by computer-based systems is a realistic proposition.

Research Objective and Research Questions

These directions of research were translated into the following research objective:

"To investigate the information flows of top managers in order to evaluate the validity of the concept of an information system for executives and develop guidelines for the design of future systems."

In order to meet this objective, four specific questions were asked:

1. What are the characteristics of the communication networks of executives?

2. What information do executives use and how do they add value to it?

3. What communication channels do executives use?

4. How do executives view computers and computerised information systems?

Chapter Four

Planning the Empirical Work:
Thinking about Research Methodologies

Before talking about research methodologies per se, it is useful to spend a few pages highlighting the more fundamental debate that has been taking place in most areas of research, especially in the social sciences, over the last 100 years. This debate contrasts two radically different visions of the process of inquiry that has been called 'science' and has implications for anyone who intends to undertake research. Readers who are not interested in this philosophical debate may (on the first reading) scan the next pages more rapidly and concentrate on the more practical conclusions provided at the end of this chapter regarding the selection of research methods and the planning for empirical work (see 'Where Next?' at the end of this chapter).

Philosophical Debates on the Nature of Scientific Enquiry

Kerlinger (1973) has proposed that a powerful way to understand the nature of scientific research is to compare it to another human method of making sense of day to day experiences: common sense. From this comparison, a number of basic similarities and differences emerge that allow for a specific characterisation of what science is and is not. Whitehead (1911) has noted that as far as creative thoughts are concerned, common sense is a bad master. He stated:

> Its sole criterion for judgement is that the new ideas should look like the old ones (p. 157).

Kerlinger (1973) emphasised that the differences between common sense and science stem broadly from the systematic and controlled approach to creative thinking that characterises the scientific process. In his vision, the scientist is different from the man in the street because he

> systematically builds his theoretical structures, tests them for

> internal consistency, and subjects them to empirical testing
> (p. 3).

Furthermore, the scientist,

> knowing 'selection tendency' to be a common psychological
> phenomenon, carefully guards his research against his own
> preconceptions and predilections and against selective sup-
> port for his hypotheses (p. 4).

Finally, the scientist systematically tries to rule out variables that
are possible 'causes' of the effects he is studying other than the
variables that he has hypothesised to be the causes. Thus, according to this vision of scientific research, knowledge can rigorously
emerge only through a process of systematic inquiry and in totally
controlled ways. This vision is representative of a large body of
work which has presented the method of science as the ultimate
method of knowing. Pierce (in Buchler, 1955) has provided a formal definition for this method:

> To satisfy our doubts, therefore, it is necessary that a method
> should be found by which our beliefs may be determined by
> nothing human, but by some external permanency – by some-
> thing upon which our thinking has no effect. . . . The method
> must be such that the conclusions of every man shall be the
> same. Such is the method of science. Its fundamental hypoth-
> esis . . . is this: there are real things, whose characters are
> entirely independent from our opinions (p. 18).

However, a scan of the literature relevant to human experiences
with science and scientific investigation quickly indicates the existence of alternative visions of the scientific process, which are
inconsistent with the above definition. Other researchers, perhaps
less concerned with the pedagogic nature of their explanations, have
presented a radically different vision of scientific research which
emphasised the very human nature of this activity rather than its
systematic and controlled nature (McGrath *et al.*, 1982). Thus,
McGrath (1982) has suggested that science must also be characterised by the judgment calls that researchers must make on a day to
day basis when they practice research. Specifically, he defined these
judgment calls as

> all of those decisions (some big, some small, but all neces-
> sary and consequential) that must be made without the ben-

efits of a fixed, 'objective' rule that one can apply, with precision, like a template or a pair of callipers (p. 13).

Highlighting that he borrowed this term from baseball, he indicated how, in this game,

such judgement calls accumulate in their effects; and, indeed,
they quite literally determine the outcome of most games (p.
13).

Thus, he claimed that researchers are faced with the difficult task
of making many crucial decisions likely to change the results of
their research without the benefit of a specific set of objective rules.
According to McGrath, Martin and Kulka (1982), no area of the
process of scientific inquiry escapes these judgment calls. It involves decisions made by researchers regarding the choice of a
strategy, the research design, the measurement tools, etc. This vision of the research process is obviously at odds with the definition
proposed by Pierce, who viewed the scientific process as purely
systematic and devoid of anything human. Clearly, these two visions cannot be reconciled and indicate very deep philosophical
differences that have split researchers across fields of inquiry.

In addition, Martin (1982) has noted that the research process as
it really takes place is far less orderly than has been reported in
many a manual or textbook on research methods. She contends
that the garbage can metaphor of Cohen *et al.* (1972) might be a
more realistic model to describe the process of social inquiry than
most of the 'rational' models put forward by previous researchers
(e.g. Selltiz *et al.*, 1959). Based on her experience of carrying out
research in social sciences, Martin (1982) highlighted a number of
myths of research processes that she derived from the rational models of research and from counter-examples emerging from her garbage can model. These unrealistic, idealised standards of research
include the following assumptions:

- resources are only important as enablers of the research process;

- the nature of the theoretical problem determines the choice of
methodology;

- the choice of a methodology has no bearing on the results of the
research;

- results are suitably looked at as the endpoint of the research process, as opposed to the start point.

Based on these observations, Martin proposed a more practical vision of the research process that leaves room for serendipitous discoveries, theoretical orientation constrained by the necessity of obtaining funding, choice of a methodology based on available means and current expertise of the researcher and other characteristics of actual research projects rather than claiming allegiance to more 'acceptable' normative models that were not respected. Kulka (1982) provided many examples of the kind of difficulties into which many previous researchers ran and the actual reasons they used to make their judgment calls. In particular, he quoted Browne (1976), who proposed the following set of criteria for his selection of a group to study:

> To my way of thinking, there are four reasons for choosing one group over another: the group should be fun, accessible, convenient and suitable. Lest these criteria be dismissed as frivolous, let me explain. Fieldwork is exhausting, difficult, psychologically demanding and time consuming. The more fun and interesting the group, the greater the likelihood that your interest and commitment will be sustained. A fun group can be just as important as a dull group, and a lot easier to study (p. 56).

Moore (1977) described the process he used to select his informants in the following terms:

> . . . my meetings with people were based on introductions from friends and relatives or were haphazard; I approached organisations through their officers. How typical, in the statistical sense, were the people I had met? How widely held were the views I had heard expressed in cafes, pubs and churches? Did my face or my manner invite particular kinds of meetings or evoke particular opinions (p. 55)?

This accumulation of accidents and irregularities in the experiences of actual researchers lends much support to the garbage can vision of the research process put forward by Martin (1982). By all accounts, Kulka's reference to the chaos of research projects seems hardly exaggerated.

In the final analysis, the fundamental difference between these experiences of the process of scientific inquiry boils down to one crucial belief that on the one hand, social inquiry can be regulated formally in a generic fashion, or on the other hand, that

> one loses a great deal when one attempts to fashion sound research entirely on the basis of general decision rules routinely applied (McGrath, 1982; p. 14).

For the purposes of this book, we will be satisfied with having highlighted this basic conflict between different perspectives on research: one which regards science as essentially objective, i.e., anchored in a reality lying outside of the scientist and his or her personal beliefs, perceptions, biases, values, attitudes and emotions, and the other one which emphasises the existence of crucial judgment calls within the research process requiring that the researcher's unique skills, resources and purposes be brought to bear. Students must be aware of this debate and make up their minds as to what school of thought they want to adhere to. Alternatively, they might decide that these high-level debates do not matter and that an ad hoc approach is more suited to their needs. All of these choices are acceptable as long as they are made from a position of knowledge and not by default or from a position of ignorance.

To clarify this controversy, it is useful to explain that the multitude of visions and experiences of the process of research is best analysed by taking one step back and considering the philosophical differences underlying these visions. There has been a general debate in the social sciences regarding the philosophical reference that should guide research in a general sense, and authors have commonly identified two main traditions. Walker (1985) has found that these antagonistic frames of reference have been labelled in many different ways, including positivistic and humanistic (Hughes, 1976), positivistic and interpretative (Giddens, 1976), scientific and humanistic (Martindale, 1974) or naturalistic and humanistic (Poloma, 1979). Other authors have also referred to objective versus subjective research (Burrell and Morgan, 1979) and monothetic versus idiographic (Luthans and Davis, 1982). In this book, these two traditions are referred to as positivist and interpretivist, terms that suitably describe the philosophical orientation of both paradigms. Students can refer to the guide to the ideas that shaped research in Part Two in order to find robust definitions for some of these terms.

Research Traditions in the Social Sciences

The positivist and interpretivist traditions which we have introduced in the previous paragraphs have commonly been associated respectively with the physical sciences, such as physics or chemistry, and the social sciences, such as sociology (perhaps the oldest of social sciences) or psychology. Clearly, there are some fundamental differences between both approaches. Researchers who adopted one of these often argue vigorously against the other and the existence of these two paradigms reflects more than just the fundamental differences between the social sciences and the physical sciences. In fact, the debate has taken place within most social sciences, in particular in sociology. In this area, Dumont and Wilson (1967) have claimed that sociologists who refute the applicability of criteria for validation of research used in the physical sciences to their research confuse technique and methodology. Rudner (1966) has stated that

> the methodology of scientific discipline is not a matter of its transient techniques but of its logic of justification. The method of science is, indeed, the rationale on which it bases its acceptance or rejection of hypotheses and theories. Accordingly, to hold that the social sciences are methodologically distinct from the non-social sciences is to hold not merely (or perhaps not at all) the banal view that the social sciences employ different techniques of inquiry, but rather the startling view that the social sciences require a different logic of inquiry. To hold such a view, moreover, is to deny that all of science is characterised by a common logic of justification in its acceptance or rejection of hypotheses (p. 5).

This statement implies a clear rejection of any alternative (non-positivist) paradigmatic position in the social sciences. This shows that this debate is far from limited to an opposition between the social and physical fields of inquiry. However, researchers have more recently become convinced that there are indeed some fundamental differences between the inquiry that takes place in physical and non-physical fields (Guba and Lincoln, 1994; Schwandt, 1994). They have identified that the problems of social sciences stem primarily from the extreme complexity of the problems they address (Trigg, 1985) and the identical nature of the social scientist and the object of his or her research (Todorov, 1989). Specifically, it seems that the physical sciences do not raise the same philosophical problems that researchers face in the practice of social sciences. As noted by Trigg (1985),

> We cannot look at human society without some conception of human nature. I cannot become a social scientist without facing the question who 'I' am. This constitutes a radical difference from physical science. It is possible to study the behaviour of material objects without being constantly brought face to face with myself (p. 205).

Todorov (1989) added that it is not interesting to oppose the human sciences and the natural ones based on the degree of accuracy in the results on the nature of the mental operations involved or on the conditions of observation. He claimed that the fundamental difference in the subject of the study (i.e. human/non-human) is followed by another, more critical, difference: the nature of the relationship between the scientist and the objects of his or her inquiry. He stated,

> So many things separate the geologist from his minerals, whereas the historian or the psychologist are very near their objects: other human beings. It does not mean that researchers in these areas aspire to less accuracy or refuse the principles of reason, but that they refuse to eliminate what makes the specificity of the social sciences: the community of the subject and the object and the inescapable intertwining of the facts and the values (p. 10).[1]

Another source of difference for researchers in human behaviour is the extreme difficulty in objectively interpreting findings of a 'soft' nature. The field of ethnology is rife with instances of serious studies into the same phenomena reporting conflicting findings (Bryman, 1988). Redfield (1930) and Lewis (1951) studied the same Mexican village nineteen years apart with the former concluding that the village was a harmonious, conflict-free and well integrated environment, and the latter that it was ridden with fear, conflict, individualism and divisions. In a (later) effort to clarify this discrepancy, Redfield concluded that he had attempted to answer the question, "What do these people enjoy?" while Lewis tried to answer

---

[1] Translated from French by the authors.

the question "What do these people suffer from?" Even more difficult to explain were the differences found by Slater's (1976) and
Gartrell's (1979) studies of populations in southwestern Tanzania,
the former reporting these populations to be 'like zombies', reti-
cent and hostile while the latter found them to be warm, generous
and open.

Foundations for a Paradigm for Business Research in the 1990s: Looking at the Example of Information Systems

This debate regarding the most suitable paradigm to apply to research in the Social Sciences has specific parallels in the IS field.
Authors have been wondering about the nature of the research carried out by IS researchers and about the applicability of existing
paradigms to the IS field. The membership of IS in the realm of
social sciences is no longer debated and points to the importance
of qualitative oriented research methods for inquiry related to the
development of information systems or the usage of information in
organisations.

Thus, the debate that considers which paradigmatic tradition is
best suited for inquiry in the IS field must be informed by a reflec-
tion on the nature of this inquiry. Specifically, the questions put
forward by Trigg (1985) and Todorov (1989) about the relationship between the researcher and the objects of his or her study must
be answered by each individual researcher in view of the goals
they are pursuing so that a paradigm and a set of methods can emerge
to guide the research process.

Guba and Lincoln (1994) proposed a formalised sequence of
questions leading to a fuller understanding of the consequences of
researchers making choices in relation to the paradigmatic position they want to adopt. They suggested that a paradigm is appro-
priately described as a set of basic beliefs dealing with first principles and representing

> a worldview that defines, for its holder, the nature of the world,
> the individual's place in it and the range of possible relation-
> ships to that world and its parts (p. 107).

According to them, the beliefs are basic in the sense that they must
be accepted simply on faith (however well argued), but the beliefs
themselves constitute a legitimate domain of inquiry for research-

ers who feel they need to better understand the consequences of the choices they make. Such inquiry can be operationalised by the consideration of three fundamental questions:

1. The ontological question, which deals with the form and nature of reality, i.e. 'what is it that can be known about the world';

2. The epistemological question, which deals with the nature of the relationship between the researcher and what can be known;

3. The methodological question, which deals with the ways in which the inquirer can go about finding out what he or she believes can be known.

Table 4.1 which can easily be applied to any research project in the IS field shows the responses to these three questions that Guba and Lincoln (1994) have proposed for the main paradigms in use in contemporary social research.[2]

Table 4.1: Basic beliefs of main inquiry paradigms

Question	Positivism	Interpretivist
Ontological	Naive realism, 'real' but apprehendable.	Relativism, local and specific constructed realities.
Epistemological	Dualist/objectivist; findings true.	Transactional/subjectivist; created findings.
Methodological	Experimental/manipulative verification of hypotheses, chiefly quantitative methods.	Hermeneutical/dialectical, mainly qualitative with support from quantitative methods.

Adapted from Guba and Lincoln (1994)

---

[2] The original table by Guba and Lincoln shows the constructivist paradigm instead of the interpretivist paradigm. For the purpose of this book, it does not seem relevant to make a specific distinction between these neighbouring paradigms. According to Schwandt (1994), these two paradigms share the goal of understanding the complex world of lived experience from the point of view of those who live it and to uncover situation-specific meanings that must then be interpreted by the researcher in his or her specific experience and frame of reference. In that sense, both are broadly interchangeable, hence our consistent use of the term interpretivist. The original table also introduces the post-positivist paradigm, but such subtle differences are beyond the scope of this book. Students who require more information should refer to the original chapter by Guba and Lincoln in Denzin *et al.* (1994).

Table 1 synthesises the key differences between the two major paradigms discussed in this chapter thus far. It highlights that the positivist paradigm assumes the existence out there of one reality independent from those who study it and which can be discovered finding per finding by stating and confirming/disproving hypotheses. It also highlights that, by contrast, the interpretivist approach posits that realities must be constructed by researchers and, in a way, are relative and specific to individual research projects taking place at a particular point in time in a particular place. It also explains how reality is objective and universal in a positivist perspective, whereas it is essentially subjective in an interpretivist perspective.

Thus, it would seem that IS researchers, like other researchers in the business area, must refuse to be drawn to an overly positivist bias in the methods they use and in the assessment of the validity of their research. In the final analysis, the most important issue is less that all areas of research share a common empirical methodology than that all areas of inquiry use methodologies which enable them to discover the nature of the reality they are investigating (Trigg, 1985). If social reality does not rest on any determinism and rests with individuals (unlike what happens with physical reality), then social scientists must use methods that are different from those used by their colleagues in physical sciences and that serve their goals in the most appropriate manner.

Research Paradigms in Managerial Accounting

Different strands of research are rooted in differing conceptions of the nature of science, and research in the area of managerial accounting is no exception in this regard. Management accounting as a discipline has been traditionally perceived as being focused on the determination of cost, and more particularly product costs, hence the links to economic theories and modes of research. Research in the 1950s and 1960s was characterised as predominantly normative, based on neo-classical economic frameworks, expanding notions of cost towards that of information for planning and control purposes.

Normative accounting research at this time concentrated on broadening the concept of 'cost' towards that of 'specific costs for specific purposes', with economic theory, and in particular agency theory, in use to analyse specific decision-making situations and determine the most appropriate cost conditions in that context. Implicit in this was the acceptance of the assumptions of neo-classical economics: identifiable, rational, profit-maximising decision-makers; certainty; and costless and complete information. Refinement of such models and of the 'answers' they offered was primarily achieved via mathematical means, summed up by Ryan *et al.* (1992) as follows:

> The major attraction of an economic framework (with its profit maximising objective) was that it permitted rigorous mathematical analysis of management accounting problems. This provided a considerable measure of academic respectability for the study of management accounting. But it also meant that on occasions mathematical elegance took precedence over practical usefulness (p. 46).

Deductive reasoning of this nature came under increasing pressures, however, as researchers sought to expand their models beyond the simplifying assumptions of such economic analysis. Consideration of uncertainty issues and of the cost/benefit trade-offs regarding information for decision-making and control led to a change in emphasis in management accounting research (Ryan *et al.*, 1992). Differences between the conventional wisdom in management accounting theory, techniques and rhetoric as taught by its academics and the actual practice of management accounting practice as observed in organisations led to a changing emphasis towards a more descriptive, empirically-based research methodology.

The need for positive theories based on empirical research concerned with the explanation and prediction of accounting practice became increasingly apparent throughout the 1970s and 1980s (Ryan *et al.*, 1992), with much debate concentrating on the relevance or otherwise of much of the existing content of established managerial accounting research (cf. Johnson and Kaplan, 1987). New developments in the environment surrounding managerial accounting facilitated this changing emphasis in research and research methodologies, with growing awareness of and interest in case-based and field-based research considering of the processes by which and through which managerial accounting seeks to act (cf. Otley, 1988; Kaplan, 1986, 1993; Hopwood, 1983). This recognition of the need to broaden the focus of the management accounting function and of associated research in the subject area has continued into the 1990s and is evidenced in the growing body of literature appearing under the umbrella of Strategic Management Accounting in both professional and academic publications (c.f. Simmonds, 1981; Bromwich, 1990; Dent, 1990; Howel and Soucy, 1990; Jayson, 1992; Wilson, 1994).

So, Conclusion So Far Are . . .

The conclusions that can be reached from this (necessarily short and incomplete) presentation of a long-term debate are that both paradigms have emerged and have been developed to their current status as leading visions of the world in response to specific needs experienced by researchers placed in various research situations. As such, both paradigms are valid and useful, albeit in different situations. Ultimately, researchers must seek to utilise the full range of research methods to maximise the effectiveness of their research designs and this can only be achieved in view of each specific research project.

Let us take the example of two classical research methods – case studies and laboratory experiments – commonly associated with the interpretivist and positivist paradigms respectively, and often said to be in opposition. The history of sciences has demonstrated that each represents a necessary and powerful 'weapon' in the arsenal of the modern researcher. In the field of psychology, Bouchard (1976) retraced the progressive accumulation of knowledge in the area of frustration-regression causal relationships. In 1941, Barker *et al.* conducted a famous laboratory experiment which established that frustration in children may lead to regression (Bouchard, 1976). Twenty years later, a field study conducted by one of Barker's students, Fawl (1963), showed little support for the original finding. Thus, the two methods yielded different kinds of knowledge: the laboratory experiment clearly demonstrated the existence of a causal link between frustration and regression, while the field study highlighted the low generalisability of the phenomenon and helped clarify the exact conditions in which it occurs, i.e. when a child cannot escape the source of the frustration and his repertoire of potential responses is very limited (Bouchard, 1976).

Thus, as the given examples demonstrate, all methods are potentially useful assuming that they are used to investigate a type of research question to which they are well suited.

Trade-offs and Criteria in the Selection of Research Designs

At a more practical level, researchers must develop a strong awareness of the possibilities offered by the methods that are available and the limitations that result from their specificities in order to be able to put together their own research strategy (McGrath, 1984; Galliers and Land, 1987). As Trow (1957) put it,

> Let us be done with the arguments of "participant observation" versus "interviewing" . . . and get on with the business of attacking our problems with the widest array of conceptual and methodological tools that we possess and they demand (p. 54).

Much progress in the social sciences has been achieved by enlarging and refining the methodological arsenal of social scientists. Simon (1980) stated that

> An important part of the history of social sciences over the past 100 years, and their prospects for the future, can be written in terms of advances in the tools for empirical observation and in the growing bodies of data produced by those tools (p. 72).

For new or would-be researchers, the recourse to presentations of these trade-offs and limitations of existing methods by more experienced researchers is the most reliable source of information about these matters, as the next section demonstrates.

Accuracy, Generalisability and Realism

McGrath (1984) has put forward a simple model to illustrate the trade-offs facing researchers in behavioural areas. Based on the assumption that available methods must be regarded as offering potential opportunities not available by other means, but also as having inherent limitations, he explained that researchers are faced with the task of creating research designs which maximise: (1) the generalisability of the evidence collected, (2) the precision of the measurement of the behaviour of the actors/objects studied and (3) the realism of the situation or context in which the evidence is collected. Naturally, such perfect designs are impossible to achieve as efforts to increase one parameter typically decrease the other two. Figure 4.1 highlights how the most common research methods fare against the three parameters identified by McGrath (1984) and indicates the degree of obtrusiveness and the potential for universal applicability of each method. This diagram is very useful in understanding the mechanisms whereby certain methods are better suited to some research projects.

The weakness of Figure 4.1 is that it does not provide a much needed breakdown of the 'field studies' category which, in itself, contains many different strategies in the business area (Galliers, 1985; Galliers and Land, 1987; Hirschheim, 1985) and in other fields (Bouchard, 1976). Indeed, researchers have noted the importance and the variety of methods under the common label 'field studies'. Most notably, these include field surveys, which have been identified as the most widely used method in the IS field (Kraemer and Dutton, 1991); case studies, which have been used very effectively in situations where the theoretical foundations available were meagre or did not enable the a priori formalisation of research issues (e.g. Sauer, 1993); and action research, where the researcher is involved to various degrees in the setting he or she is studying (Jenkins, 1985).

Applying McGrath's classification of research methods, it is possible to differentiate further between these three research strategies. Thus, surveys are more accurate than case studies because they only measure a small number of parameters but in so doing they sacrifice the realism of their results to their focus on many cases and few variables. Case studies, in contrast, are very realistic, but sacrifice the generalisability of their results to their focus on a single case (or a small number of cases in the case of multiple case studies).

Qualitative versus Quantitative Research
Another important means to differentiate and classify research methods focuses on the nature of the data that each of them enables researchers to collect. Previous researchers have commonly differentiated between qualitative and quantitative research, in which qualitative and quantitative data are collected (Guba and Lincoln,

Figure 4.1: Trade-offs of common research methods

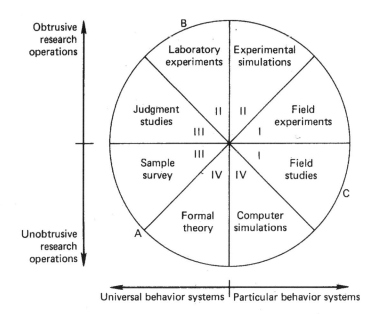

I.   Settings in natural systems.
II. Contrived and created settings.
III. Behavior not setting dependent.
IV. No observation of behavior required.
A.   Point of maximum concern with generality over actors.
B.   Point of maximum concern with precision measurement of behavior.
C.   Point of maximum concern with system character of context.

Source: McGrath (1984), p. 32.

1994; Lee, 1991; Kaplan and Duchon, 1988). Quantitatively oriented research is traditionally associated with the positivistic paradigm while qualitatively oriented research is traditionally associated with the interpretivist paradigm. Both orientations, however, can theoretically be supported under both paradigms.

Patton (1990) stated that the main difference between qualitative and quantitative research resides in the trade-off between depth and breadth. Because quantitative methods require the use of highly standardised approaches, they can handle the collection of data across very wide samples (breadth). On the other hand, they often result in fitting individuals' behaviour in pre-determined categories and the data obtained can appear very dry in comparison with the very rich data provided by qualitative studies (depth). Also, a 'context stripping' effect may sometimes result from researchers attempting to buy enough objectivity, testability and reproducibility to meet the strict canons of the positivist paradigm. That is why researchers have argued that there is a need for more context-dependent research.

Such investigations are characterised by the detailed observation of a natural setting (or possibly the involvement of the researcher in that setting) and the rejection of any prior commitment to theoretical constructs or to hypotheses formulated before entering the field (Yin, 1994). In that sense, such qualitative research attempts to use the data it collects to pose, refine and answer the research questions. This takes place through cycles of data collection and analysis whereby the understanding emerging from the data is tested until some coherent interpretation is achieved (Van Maanen, 1983). Kaplan and Duchon (1988) have noted that this process is less formalised than any quantitative research endeavour. They have reported that research processes that include qualitative approaches are inherently messy. They explained that since impressions, interpretations, propositions and hypotheses develop over the course of the study, the research process hardly fits the positivist ideal of objective collection of neutral or purely descriptive 'facts'. However, they concluded that this messiness should not dismay those who experience it (p. 582).

Glaser and Strauss (1967) have put forward a new framework for inquiry in areas where little or no understanding is available. In their perspective, which they have labelled 'grounded theory' (GT), researchers develop theoretical sensitivity prior to 'entering the field' and collect rough data without any preconceived idea until patterns and categories emerge from it. This strategy clearly requires the researchers to have tremendous skills in order to maintain a sufficient level of rigour in the research process. Recently, these two authors have split and pursued different routes in their development of grounded theory. Glaser (1992) has pushed this methodology to its extreme by claiming that researchers should read extensively *outside* their area of inquiry in order to develop their theoretical sensitivity without sacrificing their spontaneity. Alternatively,

Strauss and Corbin (1990) have attempted to codify grounded theory more precisely in order to make it practical for a wider audience of researchers not necessarily very experienced with grounded theory itself.

For would-be grounded theorists, the best advice is to read the books referenced in the paragraph above. Some initial explanation of what GT is about can nevertheless be provided. Fitzgerald (1997) proposed that the basic elements and techniques of the GT approach (in italics in the paragraphs below) can be briefly explained as follows:

- *Determining initial seed categories:* the GT approach allows researchers to enter the research process with a number of seed categories reflecting the assumptions of the research (Miles and Huberman, 1984).

- *Comparing incidents applicable to each category:* as data is collected, the method of comparative analysis is used to identify similarities and differences in the data, thereby refining the data into categories (conceptual constructs that appear pivotal and emerge from the raw data). The general term for conceptualising data is that of coding. Strauss and Corbin (1990) propose three categories of coding. Firstly, open coding is concerned with both labelling the phenomena and concepts inherent in the data, and grouping these concepts into categories. Secondly, axial coding is concerned with identifying the relationships between categories and validating these relationships in the data. Finally, selective coding is concerned with developing theory to fit the data. This results in the emergence of certain core categories which need to be related to other categories. As data is coded into categories, various theoretical questions, hypotheses and code summaries arise. These are captured in analytic memos, which are used to subsequently help integrate the theory and refine further data collection.

- *Integration of categories and their properties:* integration refers to the increasing organisation or articulation of theoretical components. This is characterised by the researcher moving from comparison of incidents within a category to comparison of incidents with the emerging properties of a category. This leads to higher-level categories as lower level categories that emerge initially are partitioned and combined. Again, this process is reflected in the refinement and elaboration of the initial framework as the research progresses.

- *Delimiting the theory:* as categories become integrated and further data collection does not tend to cause any modification of categories, but rather reinforces already-identified properties, the category can be described as theoretically saturated. At this point, some categories emerge as core categories in that they are central to the integration of the theory. This helps the theory acquire greater parsimony.

- *Writing the theory:* in this stage, the analytic memos are consolidated and core categories and their properties are used to structure the findings and their presentation and discussion.

As it stands, grounded theory, though attractive from a conceptual point of view, remains a very technical and complex undertaking for any researcher. It is at the extreme of the 'tight versus loose' continuum of research approaches (Miles and Huberman, 1994). Highly inductive, loosely designed studies are able to capture the full complexity of social phenomena, but they take disproportionate amounts of time and require great skills from the part of the researcher. As Wolcott (1982) has said, there is great merit in being open-minded and entering research settings looking for questions as well as answers, but one cannot

> embark upon research without some idea of what one is looking for and (it is) foolish not to make that quest explicit (p. 157).

Miles and Huberman (1994) noted that tighter designs can be a wiser course even though they face the dilemma of providing more economical, comparable and generalisable findings at the expense of case-sensitiveness and realism as the data has to be bent to fit the pre-study frameworks. They conclude that "the solution may well lie in avoiding the extremes" (p. 18).

It must be noted that the inquiry of complex social phenomena and organisational phenomena in particular must rely on observation and the reliable collection of large amounts of qualitative data. For example, Sauer (1993) used case studies to investigate the causes of information systems failure in organisations, a complex phenomenon of which we are still largely ignorant. According to Sauer (1993),

> the actual experience of conducting a systematic and rigorous case study brings home the complexities of the information systems process...the complex social and political web in which computing developments are undertaken becomes salient (p. 133).

This statement can be extended to apply to many investigations in the business area.

Perhaps the best way to conclude this discussion is to simply state that qualitative and quantitative research methods should be viewed as complementary rather than as competitors. Though traditionally assumed to be so on grounds of rigour and scientific application, quantitative analysis is not always 'better' than qualitative. Statistics, for example, will only show if a given factor is significant; whether it is the most significant cannot be determined. Such analysis may also omit important variables and the social setting in which the research is situated is either ignored or assumed away. A research design or strategy is basically a set of signposts to keep the researcher headed in the right direction (Miller, 1991); its components and characteristics, whether positivistic or interpretivist; qualitative or quantitative, are less important than its suitability and aptness in addressing the research objective and research questions.

Mixed Designs, Triangulation and Objectivity

Research design has been defined by Sellitz *et al.*, (1967) as

> the arrangement of conditions for collection and analysis of data in a manner that aims to combine relevance to the research process with economy in procedure (p. 50).

The choice of research strategy, therefore, is not reducible to a decision among a predefined number of methods and techniques, and the research process almost never follows the neatly ordered sequential pattern of activities presented in most research reports (Strauss, 1987). Some researchers have pointed out that the most robust research designs are not those that rely solely on one type of data. They have called for research designs that use mix strategies in order to provide the richness that is inherently part of most disciplines in the business area.

As we have said before, McGrath (1984) stated that methods should be looked at both as offering potential opportunities not available by other means and as having inherent limitations. However, in some cases the limitations of one set of tools in relation to the exploration of a specific topic can be compensated by the complementary recourse to another set of tools (Jick, 1979). Collecting different types of data from different sources and by different means results in a broader and fuller picture of the phenomenon or unit of analysis under study (Bonoma, 1985). This is the case when, for example, qualitative data is collected to complete the understanding obtained from the results of a survey, or conversely, when quantitative data is collected to confirm and generalise the findings of a case study. This gives rise to a very large number of potential research designs that usefully mix the methods available.

Introducing triangulation into the research design is one means whereby the evidence collected from one source is corroborated by evidence collected from another source, with the discrepancies emerging between the two sets of data alerting researchers to potential analytical errors. Thus, triangulation can enhance our belief that the results are valid and not a methodological artefact (Bouchard, 1976).

Jick (1979) differentiated between two types of triangulation: *within method triangulation*, which involves checking for internal consistency and reliability (i.e. the use of different techniques within one method) and the more popular *between method triangulation*, which tests the degree of external validity (i.e. consolidates the findings obtained). In one instance of triangulation, the discrepancies existing between the qualitative and the quantitative data collected led to more exploration of the case (Kaplan and Duchon, 1988). Further analysis aimed at resolving the differences then led to the use of new statistical measurements that consolidated the findings of the qualitative data. As noted by Jick (1979), divergence in the results obtained with different methods often turns into an opportunity to uncover a richer explanation of the phenomenon under study. Thus, triangulated designs constitute more holistic research vehicles, particularly good at illuminating elements of the context and able to take the researcher further down the road to generalisation.

The purpose of research is to answer questions by using procedures that increase the likelihood that the information subsequently gathered – reliable and unbiased – will be relevant to the questions asked (Sellitz *et al.*, 1967). The seemingly undisciplined procedures and flexibility in method choice available to many researchers in the areas of managerial accounting and information systems are argued as enabling such researchers to influence the situations they are studying and hence violate the principles of scientific objectivity. Thus, the novice researcher in particular must be vigilant in observing the demands of triangulation.

Assessing the Quality of a Research Design

The quality of any research design and the subsequent data analysis function is determined by the ability of the researcher to obtain the best possible combination of a number of aspects of objectivity (see Yin, 1989; 1994). These are construct validity, internal validity, reliability and external validity. Each of these elements is discussed briefly in the following paragraphs.

Construct validity refers to the establishment and use of correct operational procedures to meet the research objectives and can be increased through the use of multiple sources of evidence and the establishment of a chain of evidence (particularly in case-based projects) building towards a common set of research findings. For example, the researcher could plan on using a combination of administrative records and other documentary evidence, interviews and observation to gather data at the research site.

Internal validity relates to the establishment of causal relationships between events and conditions in the research findings and looks at the degree to which those findings correctly map the phenomenon in question (Denzin and Lincoln, 1994). Field research, for example, offers quality, depth and richness in the research findings, stressing the importance of setting, context and the subjects' frame of reference (Marshall and Rossman, 1989). Survey research offers the possibility to examine, in much less detail but in many more instances, several examples of the research entity.

Reliability is concerned with minimising any errors or bias occurring in the research project and questions the extent to which the research methodology and associated research methods generate findings that can be reproduced by another researcher. Lack of reliability can stem from a number of sources, as identified by Shaffir and Stebbins (1991). The researcher may be limited in his or her ability to gain access to all relevant aspects of the research phenomenon, or the researcher's presence may have had a reactive effect on the activities or phenomenon being studied.

External validity deals with establishing the extent to which the research methods chosen will facilitate the generation of findings that are generalisable to other settings similar to the one in which the research is to take place. External validity may rely on either statistical or analytical generalisation within the domains of managerial accounting and information systems research. Statistical generalisation refers to inferences made on the basis of a sample of empirical data; analytical generalisation works from the descriptive data gathered in the research process and is concentrated on pattern-matching, explanation-building and time-series analysis.[3]

Where Next?

Despite the seriousness of the methodological debates that sometimes rage at conferences, students may feel that they remember little from reading the previous sections. Depending upon the requirements of their masters programme they may have to produce a more or less complete essay reporting on the issues outlined above as part of their dissertation.

The issue of what methods to employ in order to investigate one's research questions remains. A number of steps can be put forward to help students progress from the literature review stage of their research to the subsequent (presumably empirical) stages. The first one of these steps is to translate the conclusions of the literature review – the outline of the research objectives – into spe-

---

[3] Pattern-matching compares the research results to those expected on the strength of previous research. Explanation-building analyses the data by building an explanation of the phenomenon through depicting a series of causal links within it. Time-series analysis matches trends in the data gathered to prespecified, theoretically significant trends in other research findings, rival trends or trends that raise questions about the internal validity of the research study (Yin, 1989; 1994).

cific research questions. There are no strict guidelines regarding the number of questions that should be investigated, but in our experience, students at the level of a masters thesis or dissertation are better to aim at answering three questions fully and competently rather than to seek to cover more areas than the scope of their extant experience and/or ability allows for.[4] What is at stake in this stage is to operationalise the study, i.e. to describe in as much detail as available at that time what answers the study is seeking to provide, how it is seeking to provide them and what empirical findings constitute acceptable results from a quality point of view.

Obviously, this description can be more or less specific, but students can be assured that the more accurately they define their questions and the mechanisms that they will use to answer them, the easier the remaining stages of the research. Thus, it may be sufficient to plan for what data will be collected and how it will be collected, but it would be very helpful to also think about how the data may be analysed and what shape or form the conclusions may take.[5]

At this stage, students should also have a definite idea of what they require in order to implement their empirical study, e.g. one or several case studies, a list of 300 addresses of companies with the name of their finance directors or a series of interviews with at least twenty marketing managers. The only missing elements in the design of the research are the research instruments that must be developed for the purpose of enabling the plan that researchers have laid out. Some studies require only one research instrument, such as a questionnaire, while others may require a combination of various methods, e.g. the use of interviews, archival documentation and observation within the more general term of 'field study' or 'case study'.[6]

---

[4] The phrase 'research question' is used to represent a specific direction of research investigated by the researcher. It is not in the same order as a simple question as asked in a questionnaire or interview. Typically, many questions will be required in order to capture sufficient data to answer one research question.

[5] This does not mean that students should have a preconceived idea of what they will find; just that they have an idea what they may find and imagine what they might do with it at that point.

[6] We use the terms 'field study' and 'case study' interchangeably throughout this text; distinctions between the terms are arguably mainly semantic, with 'case study' implying

The choice of research strategy is not reducible to a decision among a predetermined set of methods and techniques, even though that may seem to be the perception gained from reading many published articles and research reports. The methods, tools and techniques chosen will be determined by a number of characteristics: the nature of the research topic; the methods, tools and techniques traditionally used in the discipline or general subject area; the availability and accessibility of data; and the resources, including time, available to the researcher (Layder, 1993). A combination of a rigorous and systematic approach, opportunism and serendipity in tangent with the optimal use of measures towards research validity, reliability and generalisation allow the researcher to progress from the literature review process through to operationalising the research project, performing the data gathering and analysis functions (discussed in Chapter 5) and ultimately contributing to the development of theory in the topic area.

---

teaching purposes, while 'field study' implies theorising, interpretation and generalisation. Each essentially involves research in its natural setting, and so can be considered components of the more generic term 'field research'.

Chapter Five

"Doing" Research: Following the Footsteps of the Best Investigators

Based on the research questions formalised and the methods selected, the researcher must now move out in the open and find sites or sources of information from which to collect addresses, names and so on. Before the green light is given to a student to proceed to this stage, supervisors sometimes try to establish that students have 'done their homework' and that they know what they are after. Supervisors might be afraid that students invest a lot of time or 'waste' useful contacts in trying to implement their research studies without a robust framework. Students should therefore proactively seek to demonstrate that they have reached the stage where they are ready to proceed to the empirical stages of their research.

Research Methodologies in Action

The empirical stages of any research project involve the first 'moment of truth' that the researcher will face. The chosen research instruments must be developed for the purposes of enabling the plan of research that has been laid out via the literature review and methodology chapters to go ahead. Some studies require only one research instrument, such as a questionnaire, while others may require more invention and creativity on the part of the researcher.

Returning to one of the examples used throughout the previous chapters is useful in illustrating this point. To investigate the information flows of top executives, the researcher needed to put some thought into the mechanisms he was going to use to rigorously and reliably collect data about the flows of information used by managers. About twenty interviews had to be carried out with high-level managers in a number of organisations. The researcher was uncertain how to code their resultant descriptions of the circulation of information around them and their usage of that information. The analysis of the managers' use of communication channels was also a significant avenue of research that needed attention.

Three specific research instruments were developed prior to interviewing anyone. They were:

1. an outline questionnaire that was going to be used to guide the semi-structured interviews;

2. a blank map of managers' informational positions;

3. a blank framework for analysis of managers' use of communication channels.

The questionnaire contained two types of questions: questions that concentrated on guiding the interviewees in their use of the other two research instruments and questions that focused on capturing data about the value adding activities of managers in relation to the information circulating in their organisation. Figure 5.1 shows a copy of the map listed as (2) above after it was used in one of the interviews. Figure 5.2 shows the framework listed as (3) above after it was used in another interview.

The typed elements in Figure 5.1 represent the initial framework and the handwritten 'mess' that has been added to it represent the coding of the results of the interview with that particular executive. The usefulness of this purposely designed research instrument is clear in that taking notes during the interviews to capture the information coded on the maps that emerged from the interviews would have been impossible. Some of the richness would have been lost, or at the very least, making comparisons between the different interviews would have been rather difficult. The maps proved very successful in the discussions with managers because the interviewees understood immediately what the researcher was looking for.

Figure 5.2 shows how a framework can be used to 'force' respondents to adapt their responses to fit to a particular format.[1] Standard categories were suggested, thus opinions could be easily compared across interviews. It is worth noting that the categories of the frame-

---

[1] One manager 'refused' to adhere to the rules set out by the researcher. He merely used the map to highlight that he had contacts in all available directions, but did not provide specific flows. This interview was very rich, but it could not be included in the later analysis. Such 'accidents' occur regularly and should not be a matter of worry. One interviewee out of sixteen was deemed acceptable in this research project.

Figure 5.1: Information network of one of the executives interviewed

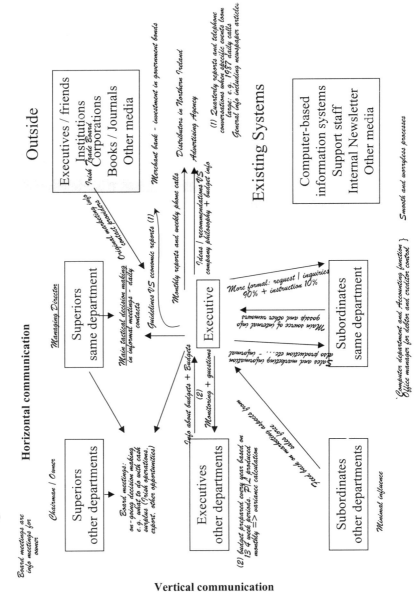

Figure 5.2: Framework for assessing the communication channel usage of one of the executives interviewed

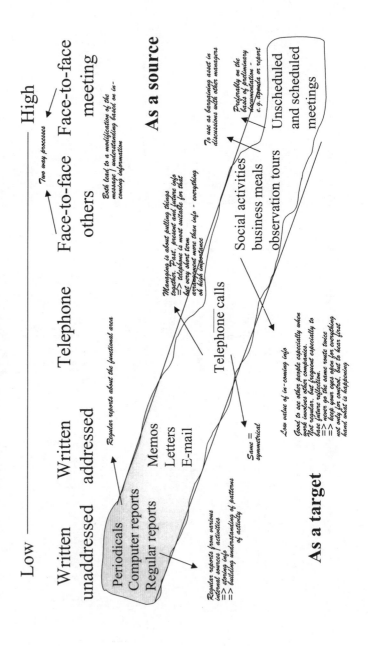

work were derived from well established sources in the literature where leading edge research on communication channels had been reported. In particular, the categories proposed by Daft and Lengel in 1984 and adopted and refined by many other researchers were used on the basis that they had been suitably validated (Daft *et al.*, 1987; Jones *et al.*, 1988). This in itself is important, as so doing facilitates the later stages of the research project whereby data gathered must be integrated with existing research on the topic, as presented in the literature review chapter(s).

The usefulness of using these two research instruments became even more obvious to the researcher when he realised the implications of not having planned for the analysis of the data collected to any formal degree. The raw data was initially a bit puzzling, but both the maps (as in Figure 5.1) and the frameworks (as in Figure 5.2) turned out to lend themselves to rigorous aggregation. Thus, the researcher realised that the maps could be analysed based on one very convenient unit of analysis[2]: the different information flows coded by the executives, broken down into in-flows and out-flows. This analysis was carried out for each map and compiled in a manner such that information from each of the interviews was condensed into a set of two tables: one depicting the in-flows and one depicting the out-flows. Figure 5.3 is an example one such table.

This example illustrates what kind of ideas can lead to an easier, more rigorous and more methodical research project. In many cases, students will not be able to plan that far ahead when they embark on their first field research (insight being a great thing in the case of the research project used here as an example), and this should not be a matter of concern. If students understand their research topics well enough and if they are careful enough in the development of their research instruments, they should obtain data that yields convincing findings related to their research questions.

Opening the Door

From a practical point of view, it is always useful to seek contacts with

---

[2] Students should note that the unit of analysis that emerged was not that originally envisaged by the researcher. However, the opportunistic nature of research in general does not preclude such changes, and indeed actually quite often leads to serendipitous discoveries well worth following.

Figure 5.3: Framework for analysis of the information flows mapped during the interview

Map number and description	Media utilised for transmission	Target of the message	Intended subject	Form of signal	Evaluation / judgement
Board Meeting	Formal	Other directors + owner	General	Hard and soft	Huge experience with company – very influential
CEO	Informal	Managing director	Strategic + general	Hard and soft	Privileged link for main corporate decision making – much value added
Monitoring of budget	Telephone and informal contact	Sales director	Budget	Soft	Negotiation
Request / inquiries and instructions	Telephone and informal contact	DP department	Sales, accounts and procedures	Soft	Privileged relationship
Guidelines for investment	Telephone and formal meeting	Banks	Goals pursued	Soft	Regular but infrequent
Company philosophy	Telephone and meeting	Advertising agency	Brand image and budget	Hard and soft	n / a

potential research 'targets' as early as possible in the life cycle of the project. Indeed, obtaining interviews or obtaining lists of potential respondents can take several weeks and significant idle time may result. This can be very frustrating, especially if students feel that they are already late in their projects and that at a later date (i.e. when they have to put together their reports and final submission deadlines are within days) they will need the time now being wasted in finding contacts. However, there is no way to avoid such problems and contacts in suitable companies or lists of addresses must be found. The luckiest students will have supervisors with good contacts in industries who can help them breach the initial resistance of managers, but in general, students will have to do the rounds and spend the time lining up opportunities for data collection. As such, the student is involved in a trade-off situation, measuring the necessity and benefits of additional data collection opportunities against the time and other resource implications of doing so. In one case, a student was already doing some work for a company that turned out to be a suitable case study. As part of his work, he collected enough information to answer his research questions. Another student spent in excess of five months obtaining interviews with IS managers and users in ten companies. She found the first few companies easily, but spent a full month chasing a few additional cases in order to comply with her supervisor's requirements. Arguably, she did waste several weeks that she could have made good use of toward the end of her project, but then these extra interviews added much quality to the research and she might not have been successful with her submission without the extra empirical work.

The difficulty in gaining suitable contacts is in persuading managers or any other required informants to give time to an interviewer or to answer a questionnaire (examples of initial contact approaches and some useful tips are presented in Part Two of this book). There are a number of methods that can be used in an attempt to boost one's chances of convincing enough informants to donate their time, as discussed below.

As far as questionnaires are concerned, the first and most important step is to put together the right questionnaire. The response rate of a survey can be determined in no small way by the length, clarity and structure of the documents sent to potential respondents. Putting together a good questionnaire is very difficult and requires a lot of experience. A thorough understanding of the research questions and how they contribute to the aims of the study is required, but consideration must also be given to the profile of the targets of the questionnaire and how much they know and don't know. In very simple terms, you cannot (and should not) ask "a cat to bark" and there are questions that should not be included in questionnaires, either because no one will answer them or because the basis for the respondents' beliefs in relation to that particular issue would be inherently biased or purely speculative. This point is worth considering because it has far-reaching implications for the design of questionnaires.

Firstly, students should select their targets carefully. Sometimes the target will be composite and include different categories of organisational actors in an attempt to either obtain a broader range of findings or corroborate the data provided by one group with the data provided by another group. A classical example in IS research is to target both systems developers and end users in order to compare and contrast their respective opinions and perceptions. The different groups may be sent either the same or slightly different questionnaires to suit their different outlooks.

Obtaining the help of an experienced researcher is always going to be an advantage and a number of face to face sessions with the supervisor or any other researcher willing to help will lead to crucial incremental improvements in any questionnaire. Yet once these initial improvements have been gained, nothing will replace a pilot survey of four or five trusted respondents. This may be seen as a waste of good contacts, as the results from the pilot normally cannot be used (since the questionnaire is changed before the main survey takes place), but there is no greater peril than sending a bad questionnaire to 300 individuals and discovering that all of them have consistently misinterpreted entire sections of the questionnaire. A pilot of five respondents should ensure that the vast majority of other respondents tackle the questionnaire as intended by the researcher and that results are valid.

Accompanying each questionnaire, there should be a brief letter of introduction outlining who the researcher is and what the general purpose of the research is concerned with (see Part Two for some helpful tips and examples). In order to increase the response rate, it is also customary to give respondents the opportunity to obtain a copy of the findings. This is usually done in the shape of an extra question at the end of the questionnaire. The effect of such a move is difficult to establish, but it can be particularly useful when trying to implement a two-stage methodology which, for example, seeks to confirm or refine survey results with interviews. Respondents who are said to be interested in the results (and have forgone their anonymity by providing their contact information[3]) can be contacted, in preference to those less interested, to enquire whether they would be willing to talk to the researcher (this can also be done upfront as an extra question in the questionnaire).

Students who want to undertake survey-based research must consider the administration of surveys. Postal surveys are more common, but electronic mail surveys can also be envisaged when the targeted population is technologically well equipped (e.g. managers in most industries). Students should pay particular attention to the issues of sampling (which is well covered in Patton, 1990 and deVaus, 1994) and non-response analysis (which is well covered in Miller, 1991 and deVaus, 1994). Ultimately, students who are trying to do a survey must remember that statistical analysis can only be used once a critical number of responses are available. Typically, more than 100 valid questionnaires should be analysed (students can expect to have to discard a few responses) and analysis should be avoided within categories where the number of respondents is too low. In this context, 100 must really be regarded as a minimal figure and any improvements on this threshold will considerably strengthen the statistical analysis applied to the data. The point is that lower numbers of observations result in each percentage point representing a fraction of the unit of analysis, e.g. one manager accounts for 5 per cent if only twenty responses were analysed. In such a scenario, a difference of four responses (possibly not very significant) can result in a disproportionately high perceived difference of 20 per cent.

This opens the door to patterns of response resulting solely from unrepresentative samples being analysed as very significant results. The example of a researcher studying the likelihood of several coins to fall on either side illustrates this last point. If the number of observations

---

[3] Questionnaires are totally anonymous when they come back from the respondents unless they have voluntarily provided contact information on the questionnaire. If they have not, the post mark is the only information available. Techniques exist that allow researchers to identify respondents (such as the use of micro-codes printed at the bottom of the questionnaires sent out), but they must be regarded as unethical if respondents are told that their responses are anonymous.

was too low, the researcher would probably reach the conclusion that some of the coins are badly made and that their centre of gravity makes them more likely to fall on one side. It is a proven occurrence (and one which students can easily experiment with, if interested!) that a local pattern can emerge that shows a coin to be more likely to fall on one side even though a much larger number of observations would confirm that the likelihood of falling on either side is 50 per cent (as expected!). Thus, students who undertake surveys must attempt to maximise the number of responses they will get. Starting from a large list of potential respondents is therefore a requirement, as response rates rarely break the 25 per cent barrier (although very topical surveys may reach higher rates).

Regarding interviews, other strategies may be pursued in order to maximise the number of potential informants. The ideal way is to identify a gatekeeper, preferably a manager who would be known either by the student or a member of staff of his or her university department, and to get in contact with him or her, informally at first in order to find out whether any unknown obstacles exist to the study and who the most appropriate person to talk to in the organisation is. The kind of inside knowledge that can be gained in this manner is invaluable, as a number of examples can illustrate. A student at our university was in the process of approaching an organisation well known locally as having been very active in developing their commercial usage of the Internet (which was at the core of his research project). A lecturer in another department of the university had done some work for the managing director of that organisation. After an informal inquiry to the managing director, the message that came back was unambiguous: two conflicting factions had emerged within the board of directors and two parallel organisations were creating themselves within the company, each with a full set of competing functional areas. The advice of the MD was clear: stay well away from that mess for fear of being dragged into a war zone, where the student might be used to provide ammunition for one side against the other, with the results of the research being unusable at the end. Having this piece of insider information saved considerable time and effort to the student and also saved him from potential trouble. The relevance of this example should not be underestimated: tense political situations develop in many organisations and it is not always visible from the outside.

Once a gatekeeper has been identified and the initial contacts are favourable, students can start asking for names of people to interview and planning for a few site visits. Depending upon the level of targeted organisational actors and the nature of the research study, the gatekeeper might have to refer the matter to high-level managers or to the managing director if access to sensitive data or sensitive organisational processes is required. In one case, one of the authors sought to study the role of IS staff in a semi-state body operating on a market that was being deregulated. Initial contacts were made with the IS director, but clearance had to be sought at the highest level because of the very tense negotiations with trade unions that were taking place at the time. Access was then granted on the condition that any publication arising from the research would be formally reviewed by the IS director for approval.

In relation to obtaining ongoing access, students should seek to clarify two issues from the earliest possible point in the research process:

1. conditions regarding access in general to the organisation and later access to particular pieces and formats of information;

2. conditions and protocols to be observed regarding the subsequent use of the data and information collected.

Clarification of these issues can be key to avoiding disagreements and disputes, and ideally should occur as early as possible in the research relationship. Students may find it useful to enlist the gatekeeper as more than just the means of access, but also as the organisational agent in relation to permission to use any data gathered. At all stages, students should behave in an ethical manner and respect the organisations' wishes, regardless of how reasonable or otherwise they many seem. Seemingly insurmountable obstacles to the use of 'good' data can be overcome through the use of non-disclosure documents (see Part Two), agreements to disguise the company / key informants and other such measures. Informants who are unwilling to be quoted verbatim in a research report may have no objection to their remarks being properly paraphrased.

At this stage, it is always useful to envisage what potential benefits will accrue to the organisation as the study is being carried out. Some important organisational processes or market research might be documented by the researcher (free of charge) and presented as a separate business report, or access might be traded against precious information on leading edge technologies that no one in the organisation knows about or has had significant time to research. In many cases, these benefits will be rather small and not very significant at the level of the organisation studied, but it is good practice to always insist on attempting to contribute something in return for the time spent with the researcher. In our experience, many managers are normally quite interested in talking to young researchers and happy to contribute to their research within reasonable time conditions once no stumbling blocks of the kind mentioned in the previous paragraphs exist. Identifying a suitable site and a friendly (but powerful) gatekeeper are often the hardest part – the rest is comparatively easy.

A more negative aspect of the issue of site selection must also be considered. Some sites where initial contacts are good can backfire and turn into time-wasting exercises. There is a trade-off between deciding to abandon a site as soon as problems start emerging or persisting for weeks without obtaining additional interviews. The best course of action is to try to minimise the negative effects of such setbacks. Thus, pursuing one or two more sites or more informants than are needed is always a good idea if you have the time and resources available to do so.

According to Miles and Huberman (1994), it is impossible to decide how many cases should be studied on statistical grounds when it comes to qualitative research. The double issue of how many cases and in what kind of sampling frame must nevertheless be answered. Patton (1990) argued that the logic underlying the sampling techniques used constitutes a fundamental difference between qualitative and quantitative research. He suggested that qualitative research and case-based research in particular must use purposive sampling methods whereby a small number of cases, or possibly just one, are selected on the basis of the information richness they will allow. More specifically, Patton (1990) isolated sixteen different purposeful sampling strategies, all based on variations of the same assumption of purposiveness. The most relevant of these different strategies and the specific purposes they serve are summarised in Table 5.1. Naturally, not all strategies can be pursued simultaneously. One must be selected on the basis of the purpose of the research.

Table 5.1: Purposeful sampling strategies

Type of Sampling Strategy	Purpose
Extreme or deviant case	Learning from highly unusual cases or manifestations of the phenomenon under study, e.g. outstanding successes or failures.
Intensity sampling	Information-rich cases that manifest the phenomenon intensely, but not extremely, e.g. good students, below average students...
Maximum variation sampling	Purposeful picking of a wide range of variations on dimensions of interest.
Homogeneous sampling	Focuses on reducing variations and simplifying analysis.
Typical case sampling	Illustrate what is normal on average.
Stratified purposeful sampling	Illustrate the characteristics of a certain subgroup of cases.
Criterion sampling	Isolate cases that meet some criterion, e.g. children who were abused in hospital.
Confirming and disconfirming cases	Elaborate and deepen initial analysis, seek exceptions and test variabilty of the phenomenon.
Opportunistic sampling	Follow new leads during fieldwork, take advantage of the unexpected.
Convenience sampling	Attempt to save time, money and effort; poor rationale.

Adapted from Patton (1990)

In addition to the issue of purposive sampling, the issue of sample size must be considered. As stated above, sample size in qualitative inquiry does not have to follow the rules of probabilistic sampling because no claim is made that the cases selected are statistically representative of a population (Patton, 1990). Patton stated clearly that there are no rules for sample size in qualitative inquiry. Sample size depends on what you want to know, the purpose of the inquiry, what's at stake, what will be useful, what will have credibility, and what can be done within available time and resources (Patton, 1990; p. 184).

Lincoln and Guba (1985) proposed a more specific criterion to judge when a suitable sample size has been achieved. They suggested that the termination of a study is determined by its informational needs: when no new information is uncovered in additional cases and all additional data collected becomes redundant, the sample size can be considered to be sufficient. This is reminiscent of the guidelines put forward by the proponents of grounded theory, whereby categories are determined and validated by theoretical saturation (see page 50). This must therefore be negotiated between the researcher(s) and the other stakeholders of the research project as the project unfolds and the findings become available. It must be noted that such a loose criterion for the termination of the fieldwork can lead to an ongoing study covering many years of work. Some overall control mechanism must therefore be put in place in order to monitor the progress of the research project and set its boundaries.

A Framework to Show Progress

One specific framework that the authors of this book use on a regular basis in their supervision can help students succeed in developing well formalised research projects at an early stage in the life cycle of the research process. The framework involves presenting the research questions (at a high level and then at lower sub-levels), the sources of data and the informants used for the research in a single table and constitutes a very convincing and complete vehicle to present a research project. It can be used in discussions with supervisors and in discussions with potential interviewees (so that they accept to take part in the study). It also provides a very easy way of monitoring the progression of the research project, and whether or not additional tools will need to be employed in collecting the required data. Table 5.2 presents a recent example of the use of the framework.

In this example the researcher is seeking to establish the true contribution of IS staff in the development of a strategic initiative in a large financial institution. Because of the difficulty of the project, the student was asked to demonstrate that he had given sufficient thought to the operationalisation of his study. An abstract of the framework he submitted is presented in Table 5.2 (this abstract represents a segment of the table which covers one of the research questions). Any student trying to justify the rationale of their proposed study and to demonstrate their preparedness to move to the next stage of the research process can use such a framework. Another critical use of this framework is in

Table 5.2: Abstract from a study framework

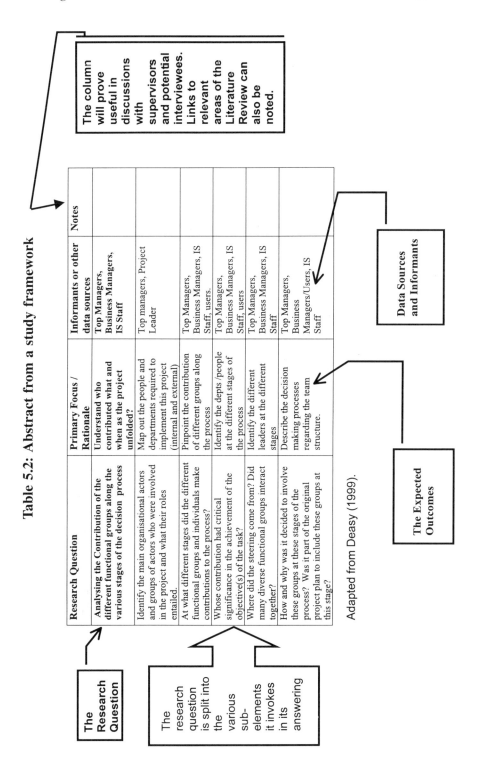

Research Question	Primary Focus / Rationale	Informants or other data sources	Notes
Analysing the Contribution of the different functional groups along the various stages of the decision process	**Understand who contributed what and when as the project unfolded?**	**Top Managers, Business Managers, IS Staff**	
Identify the main organisational actors and groups of actors who were involved in the project and what their roles entailed.	Map out the people and departments required to implement this project (internal and external)	Top managers, Project Leader	
At what different stages did the different functional groups and individuals make contributions to the process?	Pinpoint the contribution of different groups along the process	Top Managers, Business Managers, IS Staff, users.	
Whose contribution had critical significance in the achievement of the objective(s) of the task?	Identify the depts /people at the different stages of the process	Top Managers, Business Managers, IS Staff, users	
Where did the steering come from? Did many diverse functional groups interact together?	Identify the different leaders at the different stages	Top Managers, Business Managers, IS Staff	
How and why was it decided to involve these groups at these stages of the process? Was it part of the original project plan to include these groups at this stage?	Describe the decision making processes regarding the team structure.	Top Managers, Business Managers/Users, IS Staff	

Adapted from Deasy (1999).

The column will prove useful in discussions with supervisors and potential interviewees. Links to relevant areas of the Literature Review can also be noted.

The Research Question

The research question is split into the various sub-elements it invokes in its answering

Data Sources and Informants

The Expected Outcomes

establishing retrospectively that the study has been completed successfully. In other words, students who manage to address all the questions in their research framework can be satisfied that they have achieved their aims. The framework itself can be included in the final research report. It will add robustness to the study and its findings in that it will demonstrate that a rigorous research project was undertaken and that it yielded definitive answers to the questions asked by the researcher. Once students have received the approval from their supervisors, they can then use the framework itself or simply a one page document based on it to introduce external parties to their study without having to spend time preparing additional 'presentation documents' or trying to explain complicated research goals over the phone to mildly interested managers.

Collecting Data

Field research is the dominant methodological approach to postgraduate research in the general business area; thus, in the coming discussion on collecting data, survey and interview instruments are the obvious foci. While these are not the only instruments used, they are perhaps the least thought (and taught) about and perhaps the most in need of consideration by novice researchers. The main difference between field studies that use interviews and case studies, and surveys is that once the questionnaires have been posted, researchers may take a bit of a break as data starts pouring in with every day's post, whereas interviewers face a very difficult stage of their research. That said, however, the survey researcher has already put much work into the preparation of the now-posted document.

Survey Research

This does not mean that survey researchers have it easier than others do. Much risk is involved in survey research and the authors of this book are aware of a number of projects that went wrong because of the very small response rate they generated. In one instance, a study of rapid application development (RAD) in Ireland received 37 responses despite a sample population of several hundreds. Even within this small tally of responses, a third of organisations had not used RAD in any way, which made the results of the survey very insignificant. In another case, an e-mail survey of Lotus Notes users attracted an initial batch of ten responses. It took the student three months of intensely scanning the Internet and a brass neck (sneaking into a Lotus Notes discussion group to locate some potential respondents and getting some very nasty e-mails in the process) to bring the total up to fifty responses, which just about saved the day.

Getting more responses than expected can also turn into a mixed blessing as the envelopes pile up and the novice researcher wonders what to do with all that paper. Ideally, a proper retrieval matrix should be created in a statistical package, such as SPSS™, and the data should be keyed in as the questionnaires come in. More work must also be done during this period: researchers should keep track of the number of questionnaires that come each day and, more importantly, of the sequence in which they arrive. Indeed, the identification of early responses versus late responses is a crucial piece of data in measuring non-response bias. The term non-response refers to the fact that not all potential respondents replied to the survey. This is unavoidable, but researchers must ensure that it has no side effects in terms of the results of the survey. Bias can occur when respondents who would have differed markedly from the general case decide not to take part in the study. For example, in a study of disaster planning for computer systems, one would expect that IS managers who have no plan would be much slower to respond than IS managers who have a well-tested plan. This bias would result in the study reaching the conclusion that a high percentage of IS managers have an IS security plan, when in fact, those who had no plan simply did not take part in the study. One way to test for such bias is to use late respondents as surrogates for non-respondents and to compare their response to a random sample of respondents. Significant differences between the two groups may indicate a non-response bias (see Oppenheim, 1996 and Wallace and Mellor, 1988 for a more specific discussion of how this should be done).

The issue of non-respondent bias deserves additional comments. It is our experience that students (and mature researchers alike) often misunderstand the meaning of such biases in their results. Their initial reaction is often to attempt to conceal the biases they have identified (even if this means removing the test results from the research report, or even worse, falsifying the mathematical calculations so that bias will appear smaller than it really is). In fact, non-response bias is a key finding in any survey and it may be used to provide richer explanations for patterns of results that cannot easily be explained or to explain divergent results between different surveys. To be clear on this point, the discovery of strong non-respondent bias does not reflect badly on the survey and its results, but rather, it is a sign of robustness and rigour of the process followed by the researcher. It also indicates that the researcher understands the ins and outs of the techniques he or she is using. It must be measured carefully and then be used to explain why survey results are different from that of other similar surveys or to specify for what population they are particularly representative (e.g. IS managers who do undertake planning for disasters as opposed to all IS managers).

Case Studies and Interviews

Much has been written on the interview as a means to collect data for scientific purposes (Bouchard, 1976; Rubin and Rubin, 1995) and Patton (1990) has comprehensively illustrated the common biases in interviewing. Carrying out interviews, however, is not as easy as one thinks. Ultimately, interviewing boils down to walking into someone's office or into a bar (public settings of this kind rarely make it easier to interview people because of the amount of parasite noise and movement to which both interviewers and interviewees are exposed) and starting to ask questions.

By and large, researchers do not train to interview people and they hope that they will be good at it. It is nevertheless a help to rehearse at least once (maybe with another student on the programme), if only to ensure that the interviewer is suitably familiar with the questions and their sequencing. Beyond this simple training, the difficulty in interviewing informants resides in being able to conduct the interview while recording as much as possible of what is being said and done during the course of the interview. There is great peril in letting the interviewee lead the discussion by keeping one's head down and taking notes at full speed, but there is equally great danger in relying on one's memory to gather what is being said.

The use of recording devices can be considered (only with the interviewee's explicit consent), but even that does not constitute a magic bullet. Most interviews last between one and two hours, while some may last as many as four hours (some informants can be very talkative and you just cannot tell them to shut up!) and transcribing tapes is hard work. Unless you can afford to pay someone to type the contents of the tape for you, you should be ready to spend days and days typing your transcripts. In addition, some content might be lost if the quality of the recording device was not very good or if the background noise was too great. In other words, there is no substitute for a good set of notes and even researchers who tape interviews should take short notes to keep track of what's where on their tapes. Timing information is particularly useful, especially if there is no counter on your tape recorder. More specific direction in relation to taping interviews is presented in Figure 5.4.

Figure 5.4: Taping Interviews

- Taped interviews are a complement, not a substitute for taking good field notes. Allow some time in your planning to write down your impressions of the interview, important points that you noticed as it progressed, follow-on tasks or checks you need to perform and any other observations you may have.

- Obtain permission to record before the interview commences – you can explain that this will enable you to concentrate on what is being said and thus not be too distracted by note taking. Inform the interviewee that they may ask to have the recording stopped at any point if they so wish.

- Use a recorder that is unobtrusive, unthreatening and not eye-catching in appearance. Now is not the time to bring forth that super turbo power machine you bought with your first paycheque last summer!

- Check out the quality of recording in advance. Many small tape recorders produce extremely poor recordings that simply cannot be understood, particularly if they are voice-activated. This problem becomes compounded if your informants are conversing in English and it is not their first language.

- Be careful about where you place the recorder during the interview – you do not want to keep it constantly in the field of vision of an interviewee unused to being recorded; however, you must also seek to avoid any office 'noises'. Many good interviews have been lost forever because the recorder was placed unobtrusively beside the cooling fan of the desktop PC.

- Make sure that the tape is long enough to last the entire interview and that you bring plenty of spare cassettes and batteries. Just before the interview commences, record on the tape information about the date, time and person being interviewed, and any other additional information you consider relevant.

- Remember to clarify ambiguous terms, acronyms, etc. if possible directly on tape during the course of the interview, as and when they occur. Beware of 'this here' type indications when interviewees point to interesting items on the table.

- Practice beforehand with a tape recorder so that you are not afraid of the sound of your own voice in the empty silence of an interview situation.

- Always offer the interviewee a transcript of the tape and provide one as early as possible if it is requested. Respect the rights of the interviewee in that if you are asked at any point to turn off the recorder, then do so, and refrain from switching it back on again until you have obtained permission to do so. The intervening 'off the record' data can be written down immediately afterwards if you deem it important for your own impression forming. Take notes if possible.

- However, if you do turn off your tape recorder, make sure that you don't forget to turn it back on! Also make sure that the tape has not run its full course and stopped recording ten minutes ago!

- When transcribing, correct grammar, swear words, etc. unless their use in original form in quotation is a vital part of the illustration. Similar guidelines apply to using direct quotations in your research report. Always quote in context.

- Negotiate with one gatekeeper in regard to clearing materials for subsequent use. That said, however, respect the rights of each interviewee regarding that which was confidential to the interview and not for wider use in your research project.

Arguably, the obligation to take robust notes is actually a good first step in becoming very familiar with the data one must analyse. After a series of ten interviews, it can happen that the researcher struggles to remember what was said in the initial meetings. This can lead to problems if the researcher does not look at his or her notes until the fieldwork is over. Ideally, researchers should attempt to start writing their reports incrementally, or at least envisage how each interview is going to contribute to the findings. This ensures that the researcher has a good knowledge of his or her notes and that the analysis stage will not be slowed down by the researcher constantly going back and forth between the report and the notes. Needless to say, in the case where tapes have been used, the lead time in going back to any particular item that was said by an interviewee can be even greater. If you feel you need time to reflect on the data gathered during the interview (a good sign), keep the door open at the end of the interview for subsequent contact, even if only by phone or e-mail.

Other sources of data should be considered as means of triangulation. Perhaps the best rule to thumb to adopt is 'never say no' – that which you decide not to use at a later stage can be discarded.[4] This includes company documentation (such as annual reports that are always useful to write introductory sections on the organisations studied, ad hoc reports on specific projects etc.), which must always be used in an ethical manner. It is necessary to explicitly ask for permission to use such documents, to make copies of them or to show them to any third party. Very rich information can be found in such sources because they accurately reflect the philosophy of the organisation or because considerable work was involved in their compilation. In one instance, one of the authors of this book was provided with a report written by consultants on a subject that was very relevant to the study he was carrying out. In writing the report, the consultants had interviewed more than 100 staff of the organisation, a research effort that dwarfed that of the researcher! The opportunity to tap into that kind of information pool should not be ignored. Such sources must nevertheless be used ethically, e.g. be properly acknowledged. In relation to internal organisational documents, it is important to ascertain the conditions under which

---

[4]Accepting all data, documentation, etc. offered is actually quite important, particularly when using case or field study methodologies. The person offering the information obviously considers it may in some way be relevant to the research phenomenon, and thus even if you cannot see that relevance now you may in the future, at which point you would look very foolish meekly requesting that which you had earlier ignored. It may not be made available to you again as easily.

the information was gathered and its level of accuracy and suitability to your topic.

Many students also tend to ignore less obvious means of data collection, i.e. the potentially very informative conversations that can take place immediately prior to or after an interview or in the 'relaxing' time spent informally in the canteen or coffee dock. Quite often, much valuable information and personal insights can be obtained from organisational actors in such situations.

One special instance of triangulation stems from interviewing a variety of different categories of informants. This was already mentioned in the section on surveys and it is equally useful in case based research in order to corroborate the opinions and perceptions of organisational actors. Needless to say, the differences between the accounts of two interviewees must be utilised with due care. It would be unwise to antagonise one or two interviewees by pointing out that one of them must be wrong. Simple misunderstandings can be clarified at the occasion of a follow-up phone call, but it may not be possible to shed any light on more significant discrepancies. In a research study investigating the communication networks of the European subsidiary of an American multinational, the researcher discovered that the European managing director knew much more than any of his staff because he was a member of the board of directors of the US company. It also became obvious that, in some instances, he was purposefully withholding information from his managers although they would clearly have benefited from such information. This corresponds to the definition of a structural hole as described by Granovetter (1973) and Burt (1992), whereby an organisational actor distorts the circulation of information in his / her area of the organisation's communication network in order to derive benefits for him/herself. However interesting this finding might have been and however useful it would have been to push the MD and the managers in explaining why this situation was maintained, the researcher shied away from trying to find out more in order not to jeopardise a very good access to a very interesting site. The study lasted eighteen months in total and making the wrong move might have terminated it after a few months.

It is always useful to be aware of discrepancies between the perceptions of different categories of actors (even when they cannot be used in further interviews) because this knowledge makes the researcher less naïve in relation to what he or she is told by interviewees and can help avoid propaganda-like statements and official stories that are too far away from the reality of what happens in an organisation. In one case study of a semi-state company, the chairman of the board told the researcher that the company had just implemented a revolutionary customer charter, which would guarantee that customers get the best service. This customer charter was described as "useless rubbish" by one of the other directors. Although such information cannot directly be used for the purpose of interviewing, it enables the researcher to report that the customer charter is not seen as a fundamental change by all managers.

Concluding Comments

The empirical stage in a research project is the main bottleneck in terms of time elapsed. Many research projects fall behind schedule in this stage. In addition, the quality of the data collected and the reliability of the methods used to store and organise that data determine to a large extent the validity and the quality of the remaining steps in the research process. A well-designed interview agenda, for example, will also provide a means of organising, manipulating, categorising and analysing the data gathered (Marshall and Rossman, 1989). Thus, the empirical stage of a research project must be approached with special care. This time might be well spent or might be wasted, but there is little that can be done to speed up this phase in the research process. Any short cuts that are taken at this stage may have serious consequences at a later stage when incomplete information is discovered during the analysis of the data and additional interviews or questionnaires become required (with significant time implications).

In conclusion, it must be pointed out that the data collection function is a very important stage in most research projects and that it cannot be fudged or undertaken half-heartedly. It is one stage where students must endeavour to behave very ethically. In particular, they must understand that their actions *vis-à-vis* third parties can have lasting consequences not only for them, but for their supervisor and for the departments and institutions where they study as well. When proper precautions are taken and good access based on mutual trust is obtained, however, the benefits can be considerable. Students stand to learn much about what happens in organisations and to gain considerable experience that will prove invaluable to them in subsequent employment. The process and results of these research projects (especially if they are successful) will also provide an interesting topic of discussion in any job interview that might present itself. Potential employers will be impressed by a candidate who has successfully investigated an unknown organisational setting and derived specific new knowledge and experience from it.

Chapter Six

When Enough is Really Enough:
Organising and Presenting Research Data

There comes a time in the research process when both the student and the supervisor agree that enough empirical data has been collected. The number of questionnaires received is sufficient and they are of sufficient quality. The number of interviews carried out and the data they have yielded are convincing enough. At this stage, many students get the feeling that the end is near and there is some truth in this. However, much work remains to be done before seeing the chequered flag and it is very important work. This difficulty is compounded by the fact that students often feel like slowing down for a while after the tension-laden period of the empirical study. It is part of the role of the supervisor to correct any misconceptions that students might have at that stage and to state very clearly the tasks that remain to be carried out and their importance in terms of the assessment of the work overall.

It is our experience that some research projects fail to reach their full potential at this stage. In some cases, students may have written very good literature reviews and may have had very good access into an organisation. They might even have collected vast amounts of data, but they never manage to cope with the volume and richness of the data and their presentation of the empirical study is messy and unconvincing. This kind of problem can have its roots in the earlier stages of the research process if the research framework that was put forward originally was somewhat loose and thus the student fails to deal with the complexity of the research topic once the data has been collected. This stage is a real test for the research questions and the research instruments: if they fit together well, the data thus collected should also fit neatly into the research questions, and can then be used to structure the presentation of that data in a question by question format. If there are gaps, some questions that cannot be answered or some data that cannot be used within the research framework, then some reworking is required prior to any presentation or analysis of the data.

Organising Research Data

One of the key points of this stage is to establish with some certainty that enough empirical data has been collected. There is no specific test that can be applied in order to ascertain whether it is the case. In terms of surveys, the thresholds indicated in the previous chapter regarding the minimum statistical significance of the sample must apply (i.e. once more than 100 questionnaires have been received, the decoding can really begin). At the same time, it is not always a guarantee that the data collected is sufficient for the purpose of writing a dissertation. What happens if all respondents agree and no differentiating patterns of any kind emerge? What happens if Likert scales were used and all respondents picked the mid-values across all questions? In some extreme cases, the supervisor and the student may decide that additional work is required so the student is not penalised by the lack of a definite pattern in the data (which may be due more to bad luck than to bad research work *per se*). This additional work can take the shape of further interviews with some respondents aimed at refining some of the findings or confirmatory interviews with known experts in the field. One student who was investigating IS disaster and recovery planning in Ireland sought to consolidate his findings by interviewing a number of prominent IS consultants familiar with the Irish industry. These interviews did not bring much new information on the subject of disaster planning and recovery, but they were very useful in increasing confidence in the research findings and in helping the researcher get to the essence of the data he had collected.

In earlier chapters of this book, we have presented sections of a research project on executive information flows. In this case, the researcher had quite a good sense as to whether or not 'enough was enough', given the amount of empirical data that he seemed to have. However, volume is not always a sufficient indicator, and it was not until the information was organised into two tables (shown below as Tables 6.1 and 6.2) that both supervisor and student could rest assured in the knowledge that it was now 'safe' to proceed to the analysis and drafting of findings stages.

The data in each of these tables was aimed at analysing exactly what the implications of the pictures presented in earlier data gathering activities were. At all stages, the researcher found that he was much better able to consider the data once he had it organised into some form of summary format; hence the use of tables. The first attempt produced a four-column structure in the first table presented below, and from this the patterns highlighted in the two columns on the right hand side emerged (Table 6.1).

Once patterns/trends start to emerge, the biggest difficulty the researcher may have is in deciding which are the patterns worthy of additional consideration and which are best left to the wayside. The research objective and research questions developed earlier to guide the researcher represent the best means of bounding this potentially very fruitful period, and the ease with which they can be used to do so is very much related to the tightness of the research methods used. In this case, the researcher felt that it was also relevant to consider the analysis at the level of each company, given that each company represented a grouping of the individual organisational actors. The first analysis of in-flows and out-flows had shown great disparities between individual organisational actors. Analysing these disparities in terms of the companies to which managers belonged indicated that some kind of organisational culture might influence the type of communication that was established between organisational actors (Table 6.2).

In these last examples, carrying out additional interviews or data gathering activities was not compulsory from the point of view of the standard deemed necessary in the dissertation, but in other cases (i.e. where the number of questionnaires received is not sufficient or when no definitive results emerge), additional empirical work may be necessary. Such work should only be undertaken after discussions with the supervisor and *always for a justifiable reason*. In other words, additional work should not be undertaken just because it would be nice or because it is possible. A dissertation is not a normal research project where the researcher attempts to do as much as possible in order to obtain more publishable results. It is a research project, that is undertaken for the sole purpose of obtaining a master's degree and some realism must apply. Failure to acknowledge that postgraduate research must be strictly bounded in time

Table 6.1: Analysis of IF /OF ratio per manager

Job Title	Company	In-flows	Out-flows	Ratio	Category
Sales Manager*	D	--------	--------	-----	--------
Buyer	A	10	4	2.50	From 2.5 to
Finance Controller	A	7	3	2.33	1.6: more
IT Director	B	7	4	1.75	In-flows
Finance Director	B	7	4	1.75	
Training Officer	D	8	5	1.60	
Finance Director	A	9	6	1.50	From 1.5 to
HRM Director	C	8	6	1.33	1.1: more
Finance Director	D	9	7	1.29	In-flows
Finance Controller	B	5	4	1.25	
IT Director	D	6	5	1.20	
Purchasing Director	B	7	6	1.17	
Sales Director	A	7	7	1.00	Symmetrical
Finance Director	C	6	6	1.00	Structure
Production Director	C	4	5	0.80	Below 1.00:
Sales Director	C	6	8	0.75	more Out-flows
Total		106	80		
Average per actor		7.07	5.33		

*This interviewee was not happy about having to use the map, hence no scores available.

Table 6.2: Analysis of IF /OF ratio per company

Job Title	Company	In-flows	Out-flows	Ratio	Company Averages
Buyer	A	10	4	2.50	If = 8.25
Finance Controller	A	7	3	2.33	Of = 5.00
Finance Director	A	9	6	1.50	Ratio = 1.83
Sales Director	A	7	7	1.00	
IT Director	B	7	4	1.75	If = 6.5
Finance Controller	B	5	4	1.25	Of = 4.5
Finance Director	B	7	4	1.75	Ratio = 1.48
Purchasing Director	B	7	6	1.17	
Finance Director	C	6	6	1.00	If = 6.00
Production Director	C	4	5	0.80	Of = 6.25
Sales Director	C	6	8	0.75	Ratio = 0.97
HRM Director	C	8	6	1.33	
Finance Director	D	9	7	1.29	If = 7.67
Training Officer	D	8	5	1.60	Of = 5.67
IT Director	D	6	5	1.20	Ratio = 1.39
Sales Manager	D	-------	-------	-------	
Total		106	80		
Average per actor		7.07	5.33		

and aim will lead to projects that go out of control or take much longer than they should. In those cases, students must consider the implications of finishing later in terms of search for employment or even going on holidays. In other words, the marginal return of spending more time on an already satisfactory thesis must be carefully considered.

Presenting the Data

Presenting the data that has been collected is a more important step than students imagine. It is important because a thesis should be written so that someone who is not familiar with the research topic can still read the research report and understand what was attempted, what was achieved and what can be concluded from it. Thus, a reader who has not been associated with the empirical work in any way must be able to follow the reasoning behind the conclusions that are put forward and this requires that they understand the data very well. The section of the thesis that presents the data is the key to achieving this goal.

A good presentation of the data collected must basically be concise and unbiased and it must also uphold the thrust and structure of the research questions. The greatest difficulty is in putting into words patterns of data that are not always simple. This can make for very long and tedious descriptions and presentations that will bore readers rather than inform them. In many cases, tables, figures and other displays should be used whenever possible to maintain a compact and efficient style of writing. Miles and Huberman's (1994) manual on analysing data contains many excellent ideas that can be used in this stage of the research.

One parameter that influences the type of descriptions that should be undertaken is the nature of the data collected. In surveys, the mainly quantitative and well-defined nature of the data lends itself to simple descriptions on the basis of the categories used in the questionnaire (and presumably validated by previous research). The use of tables with some degree of statistical analysis and the use of charts are strongly recommended for such data so as to avoid redundant descriptions of rather evident patterns. Typically, the presentation of surveys will begin with a presentation of the *demographics of* the survey whereby the basic attributes of the respondents are accounted for. Such data is definitely best presented in tabular format, as illustrated in Table 6.3 below. One can only imagine how many paragraphs would be required to present this type of data to such a level of detail, whereas a simple table can provide all the information required by the reader in a small display.

Table 6.3: Demographic profile of organisations studied

Industry	%	(n)	Number of Employees	%	(n)	Number of Staff in IS Dept.	%	(n)
Consultant/ Software House	31	50	1 to 10	12	19	1 to 5	44	71
Gov./Public Sector/ Education	7	11	10 to 100	29	47	5 to 20	30	49
Manufacturing/ Distribution	36	58	100 to 1000	43	70	20 to 100	19	31
Wholesale/ Retail Trade	4	7	1000 to 5000	9	15	>100	7	11
Finance/ Insurance	12	19	>5000	7	11			
Services/ Communications	6	10						
Others	4	7						
Totals	100	162		100	162		100	162

Source: Fitzgerald (1998), p. 320

Patterns in data can also be illustrated with graphs of various kinds. Thus, trends can be emphasised with line charts while proportions (such as the breakdown of respondents in the different categories used) can be shown with bar charts or with pie charts (see Figure 6.1 which illustrates the breakdown of respondents in the above survey). This demographic data is important in establishing comparisons between different studies and in explaining discrepencies in results. It can also provide the basis for students to provide explanations for the results they obtain. The example presented in Figure 6.1 is particularly significant because the size of the organisation studied is often an explanatory factor for many types of research questions. Other basic attributes, such as the industry in which an organisation operates, the age of the respondents, or the number of years of experience they have in their current position, often have a reliable and well-documented explanatory power.

Figure 6.1: Breakdown of the organisations studied in Fitzgerald (1998) based on the number of staff

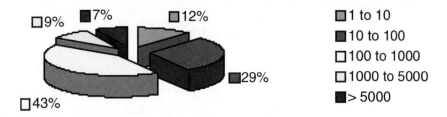

Source: Fitzgerald (1998), p. 320

The presentation of the data is more difficult when it comes to case studies and other field studies that involve large numbers of interviews. In such studies, the volume of data and their variety / disparity make it far more difficult to present them in a coherent whole and it is a real test of the robustness of the research questions to verify whether they can suitably be used for the purpose of presentation of the data.

As far as case studies are concerned, it has become a habit (at least in some areas of research) to use some sort of a narrative to introduce the case. Depending upon the unit of analysis, it can be very useful to tell the story of what happened before diving into the analysis. In a research study of managers' decision-making, the processes involved in the purchase of a large computer system became the focus of the research. The whole process took place over a period of eighteen months and was marked by a number of significant ups and downs and twists and turns that were interesting from a research point of view. In the research report, a three-page narrative was presented upfront because it was the best way that the evolution of the decision-making process could be explained to a reader outside the whole process. This was deemed to be more suitable than a cumbersome analytical description of the different stages the decision went through. This narrative is presented below.

Narrative of a Decision Making Process[1]

In March 1995, Fun Ireland Ltd, a toy company based in Ireland and the subsidiary of a large American corporation, was trying to purchase an integrated software package that would cover the financial, distribution and manufacturing aspects of their business. The business was growing rapidly on all their European markets and they were also looking into expanding into a number of South American countries. They had been a mainly manufacturing organisation, but now 75 per cent of their turnover was coming from trading goods produced by their suppliers in the Far East.

They had been reporting to their parent company the imminent failure of their current, largely manual systems for a long time, but every time they had asked for clearance to purchase any system, it had been refused by the HQ in New York. At that time, Fun only had a few PCs on which a large number of spreadsheet reports were being produced covering most aspects of the business. They also had a payroll and an inventory control system that was provided to them by a supplier of computer bureau services. However, that software and the computer running it were

---

[1] Taken from Adam, 1996. The names of the company and of the managers have been changed to facilitate reporting on the case.

now completely obsolete and Fun was the last customer using a service that was becoming more and more expensive and unreliable.

Dave, the finance director of Fun, had been wrestling with the problem ever since he had joined the company eighteen months earlier and had identified the potential failures threatening to occur in many areas. Sales order processing was his main concern as he was convinced that Fun was losing a significant portion of the ever-growing business due to orders not being met on time or being forgotten about. Yet invoicing was crucial too, and he wondered how long it would take before customers realised that Fun sometimes had no clear idea how much had been shipped to a particular customer.

After one year of work and a number of rejections from the US on technical grounds, Dave decided to hire a consultant in this area to help him produce the reports that would convince people at the HQ to give the go ahead. He got in contact with a research centre in the local university and started working with Brian, one of their researcher/lecturers.

Brian took four weeks to carry out an extensive analysis of requirements in Fun and to draw the outline of the systems required. In the report he wrote, he also pointed out the numerous weaknesses in the current systems. This report was presented to the top managers in Fun and the recommendations were approved. It was also forwarded to the HQ in the US. Brian then put together an Invitation To Tender, which was sent to six potential suppliers of systems, of which four responded within the time allocated. Based on these proposals, Brian and Dave selected two organisations with which they pursued contacts, including a formal presentation of their proposed solution and a visit of their premises. Both were local suppliers and that was largely due to Brian's perception that local support would be a very important asset during the implementation phase, as people in Fun had little experience with large computer systems (there were no IT personnel in Fun at that time). They eventually selected one supplier who made a final presentation to the top management of Fun and received the approval of the managing director. The next step was to commit the money to this investment, roughly £150,000. The signs were good when the IT director at the HQ (the one who had stopped the investment until then) responded favourably to the request and agreed with the conclusions of the final report he had been sent. All that was now needed after 20 months of the decision-making process was the signature of the finance director at the HQ.

In the meantime, Fun's parent company had purchased Kiddies Clothing Ltd, a UK-based company similar in size to Fun but operating in a complementary market. Because of the numerous uncertainties regarding the sharing of business between Fun and Kiddies and the relations to be developed between the two companies, the HQ blocked the investment in Fun.

The bad news infuriated Dave, who had put so many efforts into the whole project over a two-year period. Brian helped him find his second wind and initiated a number of meetings with equivalent personnel in Kiddies and a new strand of reports were sent to the HQ to indicate how the systems in Fun and Kiddies would inter-operate and the processes that would be shared between the two companies. A joint report signed by Fun and Kiddies was even sent to the US, which emphasised that Kiddies was ready to help Fun in their implementation of the system that Brian and Dave had selected.

Still, after two more months of negotiating with people at the HQ, the request to commit the money was rejected and the whole project put on hold while a global IT strategy for Fun was put together by the IT director at the HQ. More than two years after the first alarming reports had been written and sent to the US about the weaknesses of the current systems in Fun, nothing had been done and the manual systems were still holding on. A computerised system for Fun Ireland had never seemed so far away.

This ultimate reversal of fortune discouraged Dave, who was beginning to think that history was just going to repeat itself over and over again. Yet Brian found it difficult to accept that all the efforts of the last few months had been in vain. In an attempt to demonstrate that there were no managerial grounds for postponing any longer the commitment of Fun to the purchase of a platform and a software that had already been carefully selected, he convinced Dave and Mark (Dave's assistant) to send a final report to the HQ. In this report, they particularly emphasised that a global IT strategy for the company made little sense as no truly shared processes requiring integration of computer systems had been identified either between Ireland and the US or between Fun and Kiddies. In addition, the implementation of such global strategy meant that Fun would have to sacrifice the possibility of using local support for the software, an added difficulty for a company without full-time resident IT expertise.

Much to their surprise, this report was to win them the battle. Mid-way through December 1995, Dave got the news that he could start implementing the decision to purchase an integrated computer system covering the financial and distribution activities of Fun. Before the end of January, the cabling had been put in place and discussions were ongoing regarding the choice of a file server.

Based on such a narrative, which can readily be absorbed by a reader in a few minutes, the researcher can start analysing the situation studied as per the research questions. It is worth noting that the narrative above was the condensed version, which was presented in a paper given at a conference. Needless to say, in a thesis that concentrates on one case study, it would be quite appropriate (and even required) to spend up to five or six pages presenting a rich and catchy narrative of the event(s) on which the research is based.

Ultimately, the presentation of the case in more detail or its analysis will have to follow the structure of the research questions, especially when the research involves multiple case studies. Indeed, such research reports present an additional difficulty when the findings of the different cases are brought together. This type of research is actually quite complex (Stake, 1994). According to Stake (1994), comparison between cases is a research stage that is a conflict between learning about and learning from a particular case. He stated,

> Comparison is a powerful conceptual mechanism, fixing attention upon the few attributes being compared and obscuring other knowledge about the case (p. 242).

In addition, it appears that comparison between cases, when attempted, often narrowly focuses on the most common and general features of the organisations studied rather than devoting attention to their rich specificities. Even when systematic comparisons are undertaken within rigorous frameworks, the results are bound to be disappointing from a research point of view because there are too many ways that cases (organisations) can be different. Stake went as far as stating that

> generalisations from differences between two cases are much less to be trusted than generalisations from one (p. 242).

All researchers in the social sciences do not share this view. Miles and Huberman (1984, 1994) and Yin (1989, 1991) have described in positive terms the benefits that can be obtained by using multiple cases and cross-case analysis. Miles and Huberman (1994) have noted that cross-case analysis must first be enabled by a suitable research design. Building on arguments about the degree of tightness of the research design, they warned researchers that loose designs will make the research more receptive to the specificity of each case but will render cross-case analysis virtually impossible. Yin (1991) put forward replication strategy as one specific method to operationalise multiple case studies. In the case of replication strategies, the sampling method adopted allows the researcher to add confidence to the findings of the study. For example, by looking at a range of similar or contrasting cases, it is possible to qualify the findings obtained in one case by specifying where and how these findings apply (Miles and Huberman, 1994). Similarly, if one finding holds in cases with similar profiles but not in contrasting cases, it can be regarded as more valid and generalisable as opposed to being only grounded in one case (Yin, 1991). This does not really cancel out the inherent weakness of the case study method in relation to generalisation. In other words, the extension of the study to several cases is undertaken on conceptual grounds and not in an attempt to make the results representative of a larger population.

Perrow (1970) issued a warning to all researchers who study organisations and who try to draw conclusions from the differences they observe between the cases they study. He put forward a number of examples taken from the literature where similar organisations (i.e. organisations that are involved in the same activities) were found to be very different in the way they operate, namely whether they are successful or whether they have good or bad leaders. In particular, he described the management styles at two youth correctional facilities, one very repressive and organised and one more loosely managed and where discipline did not appear to matter so much (taken from Street, Vinter and Perrow, 1966). Outlining that these differences ran very deep in the way these two institutions were managed, he warned researchers against attempting to simplify what they see and reduce the differences to leadership styles or the personality of individuals. His analysis pointed out that

> the main difference between the two institutions appears to be the conception of the nature of the raw material with which they dealt – the delinquents – and thus what was necessary to transform this raw material. Once a definition is embedded in a program, the opinions of personnel who remain at the institution become congruent with it (Perrow, 1970; p. 34).

This analysis highlights that explaining differences between the reality of management practices in two organisations requires giving much attention to the overall philosophy (or culture, as it has sometimes been described) of each organisation and not simply to the opinions expressed by the interviewees or the individual behaviours observed by the researcher. Perrow (1970) continued his explanations of the differences between the two institutions by comparing the repressive institution with a factory where a well-mastered process is applied consistently in order to calibrate parts that need to be rehabilitated and comparing the second one with a research laboratory where unique and complex individuals are being studied by encouraging them to let go of what is at the root of their diverging behaviour in society: anger, fear, etc. Clearly, analysis at such a level requires both great attention to detail and an overall view of organisational processes.

The sampling strategy used for multiple case studies must also be considered carefully in order to create the opportunities for some degree of comparison while preserving the richness and the specificity of each individual case. This kind of balance is difficult to achieve and requires that researchers put a lot of thinking into their research framework (see Patton, 1990 on p. 75 of this book).

Using Displays for a Better Presentation

The use of display has already been put forward in the previous chapter as a powerful presentation mode that allows researchers to write compact and efficient research reports in the case when quantitative data must be explained. Yet the use of displays can really be generalised to reporting on other types of data as well. In fact, only the creativity and the imagination of the researcher limits the extent to which displays can be used. However, one essential factor should guide decision making in that area: displays should only be used if they are clear and simpler than alternative modes of presentation. In other words, researchers should not insert tables and figures for the sake of it, but only if they solve specific problems.

By and large, displays can be created to serve a number of different purposes. They can be used to bring together vast amounts of literature and to establish research questions. They can be used to present basic data (as already illustrated), to synthesise rich and complex data that is hard to grasp or to synthesise the findings of the research. The use of a display to present a synthesis of existing work can be a contribution in itself. It can be used as a structuring device for a lengthy literature review (see p. 20) or it can be used to provide richer descriptions of complex managerial processes. Figure 6.2 illustrates the types of displays that were used by a student to support his descriptions of the process of development of a large IS project. This display was presented as part of the research report corresponding to the research project already mentioned in Table 5.2. It shows the different stages that one phase of the project went through and the contribution of the different teams involved in the project. A number of icons (presented in the legend on the right hand side) have been created to symbolise the different teams and these icons were used to indicate the stage of the process where each of the teams was particularly active. Thus, Figure 6.2 can be used as a support for a written description of the interaction and collaboration between the different teams, which corresponds to the research question presented in Table 5.2 (readers can refer to this table to get some sense of how the data obtained in the interviews was coded on the diagram).

Figure 6.2: Description of a complex process using a rich diagram

Development Process of the Model for Risk Management

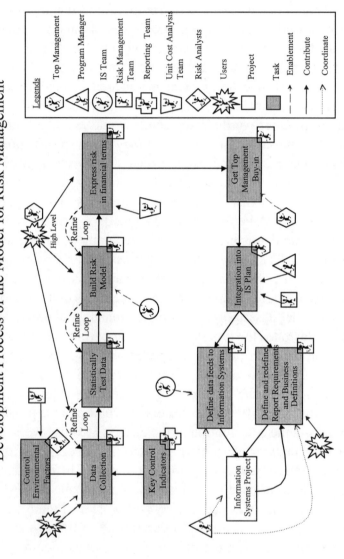

Adapted from: Deasy, 1999

Presentation versus Analysis

To conclude this chapter and perhaps to launch students on the final mile of the research marathon, we would like to sound a timely note of caution: the presentation of research data is an entirely separate task to the analysis of that data and the drafting of research findings. Students may be tempted to introduce some elements of analysis in the presentation of the data. This may or may not be suitable because on the one hand, it makes for a more compact presentation of the findings of the research, but on the other hand, it dilutes the results. A separate analysis section also makes it easier to highlight the contribution of one's research project. The data analysis phase of a research project as it will appear in the final dissertation document involves the consideration of research data after it has been organised and presented to the reader as part of the conclusions to the original research intent. It is therefore a separate exercise to simply telling the story of the research. Again, diagrams and displays are useful vehicles in organising research reports so as to achieve greater levels of clarity in presenting and analysing data and in illustrating how findings and conclusions relate to the underlying data collected. Thus, a diagram which originated in the literature review chapters (e.g. in the conclusion of the literature review) can be used as a vehicle to interpret the data collected in the research and can then be further developed in the conclusions of the study to reflect the incremental understanding and knowledge gained by the researcher. This way of organising a research report always pays dividends because it gives readers the impression that a common thread runs through the entire project and that the researcher was in control at all time (see Chapter 7, section on using displays for conceptualising conclusions).

Chapter Seven

Producing Findings that "Stick"

This next step in the research process is one which most of our students tell us is the most difficult element of the research dissertation to compile and write. It involves stating clearly what you have achieved – effectively 'nailing your colours to the mast'! This is rarely the favourite step of masters students because it comes late in the day and requires much brainwork. In fact, it can be quite puzzling initially and many students invest a lot of time before they understand what is really expected of them. For some individuals, however, this is the fun part of the process because they can use their creativity to the fullest. (Do not despair if you do not fall into this lucky bunch – just read on!) The problem is that each study obviously yields its own findings and thus no one can tell would-be researchers what their findings should be.

Students often ask their supervisors for help at this stage, but this is the stage in a research project where supervisors can (and arguably should) least contribute in specific terms. Producing findings requires an intimate knowledge of the data that only the researcher (the person who has generated the data) can reach. Supervisors can make general suggestions or may have a gut feeling about what is going to produce interesting and definitive findings, but they cannot (and arguably should not) offer too much support in producing the findings. This stage should remain a reasonably personal stage where the researcher puts his or her mark on the research process.

Finding Findings in the Data

One point that is worth restating is that the findings of a research project are necessarily hidden in the data collected. In some cases, they are not too difficult to read, as is the case in surveys where respondents can readily be fitted in predefined categories. For example, the study of IS disaster and recovery planning in Ireland mentioned in the previous chapter yielded accurate percentages of organisations who had (1) no plan whatsoever, (2) an untested plan, (3) an infrequently tested plan and (4) a regularly tested plan. However, for other researchers findings may be harder to find, or at least harder to formalise, particularly in case-based research.

In the example of the investigation of executive information flows used throughout this book, it was noted that the research instruments had yielded large volumes of data, as described in Figures 5.1, 5.2 and 5.3. The processing of the data in the maps obtained in the interviews provides an example of how basic quantitative data was derived from the data (See Tables 6.1 and 6.2 in the previous chapter). Yet the analysis of the frameworks for analysis of communication channel usage kept the researcher in the dark for much longer. Figure 5.2 shows one of the sixteen frameworks that were collected in the interviews and the researcher was initially quite uncertain as to what to do with these.

After spending quite a lot of time just looking at the figures, the researcher started creating large tables on A3 sheets in which he tried to code the totality of the data in the sixteen frameworks. One of these displays (shown in Figure 7.1) illustrates the process whereby categories can emerge. What was so interesting in this process was the way in which a specific grammar emerged from that data. Words like rare, small or vital started populating the diagram until clear patterns slowly emerged. When this was done, the researcher was able to score each column (i.e. each category of communication channel) based on a number of attributes. The figures in brackets at the bottom of each column indicate these scores. The first digit codes the number of managers who found this category of channel to be vital or important, the second digit codes the number of managers who found this category to be a potential source of information overload and the third digit codes the number of managers who thought the channels in this category were of little importance.

When tidied up, this analysis lent itself to a number of specific conclusions, as illustrated in Figure 7.2. First of all, the data indicates clearly that the first and last categories of communication channels are perceived as more useful on average than the other categories. Face to face meetings in particular get a 9 positive versus 1 negative score. They are also perceived as very useful to clarify

Figure 7.1: Basic display: all information across the sixteen interviews

Communication Channel - Overall Analysis

Name of executive	Written unaddressed	Written addressed	Telephone	Face-to-face others	Face-to-face meeting
Data removed	Intensive personal scanning = privilege data in simplest form to highlight relevance	Biggest item, but too much to manage properly time wasters - solution needed	Quite useful given the geographical spread of the company	Small	Vital for strong linkage with customers and suppliers
	Pricing file is main channel of communication	to verify that milestones have been reached - ie for specific queries only	to deal with exception or prepare a remote visit	vital source of contact with remote sites ? best way to show support	regular internal meetings
	could be better if better information and faster prepared - infrequent or very important!	quite a lot of info exchanged internally	always followed by written document	important	invaluable for cohesion especially for specific topics
	Too little time available!	mostly informal mail	0% as a target (secretary) 50% as a source mostly accidental	tours are the best way to communicate with outside labour force - systematic use of lunch and dinners as well	especially one-to-one: where you make the real discoveries!!
	Trying to organise paper-clipping service + databoard for permanent info	especially as a source - internal mail to forward documents and comments	restricted except with the sales reps - especially phone conferences - ideal to keep everyone abreast	small	30% of time: with customers and also informally - better for specific problem solving
	personal scanning for new ideas	high frequency and low value	small	crucial to obtain high value info	primary communication channel
	minor relevance (sees all reports as addressed?)	high volume	too much time spent!	insignificant	quite important
	minor relevance or crucial as a tool to bargain	quite critical by coordinating the action of the sales force	You have to type with it, but it cannot be controlled (culture)	small	30% of time ie meetings with customers - also internal but only in small groups
	small or most important source here!	small	quite important for relations with outside organisations	small	limited to major decision making to avoid time wasting
	For external info only	very rare (too formal) for the record only	quite important and most flexible to get things done	small	informal meetings are everyday tool
	too much to cope with + urgent to achieve cooperation in storing data		best for qualitative implications (especially phone conferences)	visits in remote sites are vital for efficient communication	only task forces (specific problems)
	general info	small	Super for problem solving and information gathering	infrequent	meetings should be used as a later stage in problem solving
	background only	small	secretary screens everything all the time	invaluable but cannot be used	mostly one-to-one meetings where the real work gets done
	useful on the bus!!			to initiate contacts and be polite	no way unless specific agenda!
	Important source for personal development	very important to trigger action	good for info not for action	small	Most important channel!!
	(6 | 3 | 0) but 4 for books and journals	(5 | 1 | 6)	(3 | 3 | 3)	(5 | 0 | 6)	(9 | 2 | 1) and 5 for specific problem solving

First figure: crucial; second figure: overload; third figure: little or no use specific well-defined problems. By contrast, the other categories of communication channels received mixed assessment in that equal numbers of managers thought that they were very useful or that they were not very useful. Thus, the use of these types of channels was more dependent on each manager's personal style.

Extending this analysis to the organisations to which the managers interviewed belonged (the sixteen managers belonged to four different organisations in which four interviews were carried out), it was also possible to conclude that organisations develop specific communication styles that rely more strongly upon certain channels than on others. The researcher concluded from this pattern of data that one organisation seemed to rely heavily on its internal mail and on memos, while another seemed to rely far more on unscheduled meetings, such as chance meetings in corridors.

Theory Building Stage

The function of theory in modern science is to summarise the existing state of knowledge in a given field, explain observations made in and of that field and predict the occurrence of possible future observations on the basis of the propositions contained within that theory (Sellitz *et al.*, 1967). The theory-building stage of a research project involves laying out general propositions arising from the analysis of the research data. Its purpose has been described by Kaplan (1986) as being

> to show how a variety of empirical generalisations follow logically from a small number of general propositions under certain conditions (p. 437).

The results of any research project become more meaningful when viewed as specific examples of more general propositions. The ultimate goal of the data analysis phase is to treat the evidence from the data gathering function fairly and objectively in the production of compelling conclusions and the ruling out of alternative interpretations. Data analysis brings order, structure and meaning to the mass of collected data. The purpose is not to represent the world in general, but to represent the research situation.

The data analysis function of any research project seeks to provide answers to the research questions. Interpretation searches for

Figure 7.2: Analysis of communication channels as presented in the research report

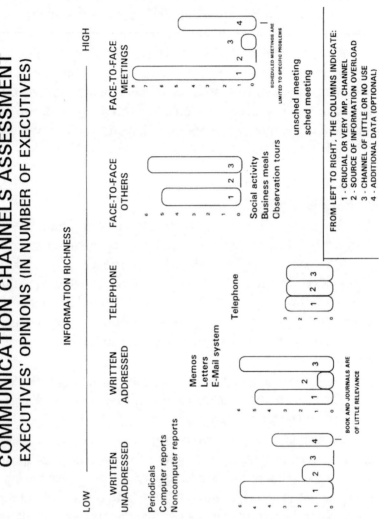

COMMUNICATION CHANNELS ASSESSMENT
EXECUTIVES' OPINIONS (IN NUMBER OF EXECUTIVES)

the broader meaning in those answers by linking them to other available knowledge and establishing a continuity in the research process over time, giving meaning to the knowledge acquired (Sellitz *et al.*, 1967). Theory thus forms

> an interface from data or observations suggesting a general principal that lies behind them as their cause, their method of operation, or their relation to other phenomenon (p. 112).

Research shapes, initiates, reformulates, defines and clarifies theory as data is collected and analysed in relation to the research questions and the overall research objective (Burgess, 1982).

The importance of theory development at the concluding stages of a research dissertation, be it theory-building, theory testing or theory extension, cannot be overstated. Incremental advances in the development of knowledge allow theories to be tested and/or expanded using data collected from different settings and at different times. Research results may serve to 'fine tune' current theoretical propositions or serve to challenge existing assumptions. Wruck (1994), for example, highlighted "change in competitive position" as being a crucial but previously forgotten intervening variable in analysing the relationship between the finance structure and market value of the organisations she studied. The need for further research on an area and a definition of the limits within which a particular theory is applicable may also be established.

The extent to which a postgraduate student can be expected to develop the theoretical contribution of his or her dissertation is primarily a function of the collective decision involving his or her supervisor and the academic requirements of the programme of study being pursued. A research report, for example, is normally far less demanding in terms of rigour in the theory-building process than is the production of a Ph.D. thesis. At a minimum, however, the findings chapter of any research report, dissertation or thesis should serve to link the research collection and analysis activities to the materials presented and arguments made in the literature review chapter(s), even if this is only done on a very superficial level. More in-depth theorising can take any of the forms mentioned in the previous paragraphs.

Given the very individual nature of a postgraduate research project, it is difficult to provide more than just these rather prescriptive paragraphs on the analysis and theoretical contribution phases of the research process. Our advice to students is to start considering the overall research project. The review of relevant literature has served to document and justify a valid research need, articulated in the form of the research objective and the research questions. The research methodology chapter has tracked the means by which these questions will be answered towards meeting that research objective, and ultimately the research need. The data collected has been organised and presented, and its analysis then serves to provide the reader with definitive statements or answers to the research questions. Unpacking these answers into a theoretical contribution is essentially showing to the reader how those now articulated answers to the research questions all 'come together' to meet the research objective.

While this may be one of the less lengthy chapters in the final product, it is definitely one of the areas most deserving of much thought. Students should realise that the bulk of the time involved in this phase is spent in discussions with their supervisor and in drafting and redrafting the 'written words' to accurately reflect the 'sense' of the research outcomes. The time necessary to do this well should not be underestimated, and neither should its importance in spelling out the implications of the research and its contribution to the field (such contribution must be attempted at a modest level if a research project is to be considered to be successful).

In Conclusion

Research results become more meaningful when viewed as specific examples of more general propositions rather than as chunks of isolated empirical evidence. 'Theoretical' does not mean 'speculative', however; a theory is still provisional in nature and may represent the most probable, efficient or consistent way of accounting for a set of research findings. It is never a static or final formulation (Sellitz *et al.*, 1967). Theory can serve to explain or predict research findings; research serves to describe and explore theory in a contextual setting. This process of reciprocal contribution is ongoing, with research stimulating theory and leading to more research. While the research findings of a project may not always be those anticipated or expected by the researcher[1], they can, in tangent with a relevant and associated theoretical base, lead to an increase in both the development and practice of knowledge.

As pointed out in the previous chapter, rich diagrams that have been developed incrementally throughout the research project can be used as support to formalise the contribution of the research. They can be presented in the conclusion of the literature review (see Figure 3.1), be used to present or illustrate some of the empirical data (see Figure 6.2) and can also be used in the conclusions to wrap up the research project in a way that highlights that the empirical data collected fit well in the research framework. This always looks more robust and can help novice researchers in putting forward a decent contribution. Such a contribution is illustrated in Figure 7.3.

In this diagram, a number of key literature review elements can be identified. The labels on the left-hand side correspond to Mintzberg's model of organisational strategy (intended, emergent and realised strategy), while the process of problem identification refers to Pounds' (1969) model, whereby managers identify problems by comparing the reality of their organisation's position and a model of where they think their organisation should be. Also, the triangle on the left-hand side corresponds to Rockart's critical success factors (CSF) methodology whereby managers articulate their vision into a set of aims which, in turn, are translated into the CSFs of the organisation. The empirical dimension of the research is integrated into the diagram in the lower left-hand corner where the model highlights how these CSFs can be articulated into a dashboard of key performance indicators measuring the distance (1) between the desired position corresponding to top managers' model and the current position of the firm, and (2) between the current position and the original position where the organisation started before the strategic initiative was implemented. A number of arrows add to this model the numerous relationships that exist between its different components. For instance, it highlights how the dashboard measures the degree to which the plans are being imple-

---

[1] Christopher Columbus, for example, set out to find a western route to the East Indies and came across the West Indies and America instead (Hakim, 1987).

Figure 7.3: Concluding a research project

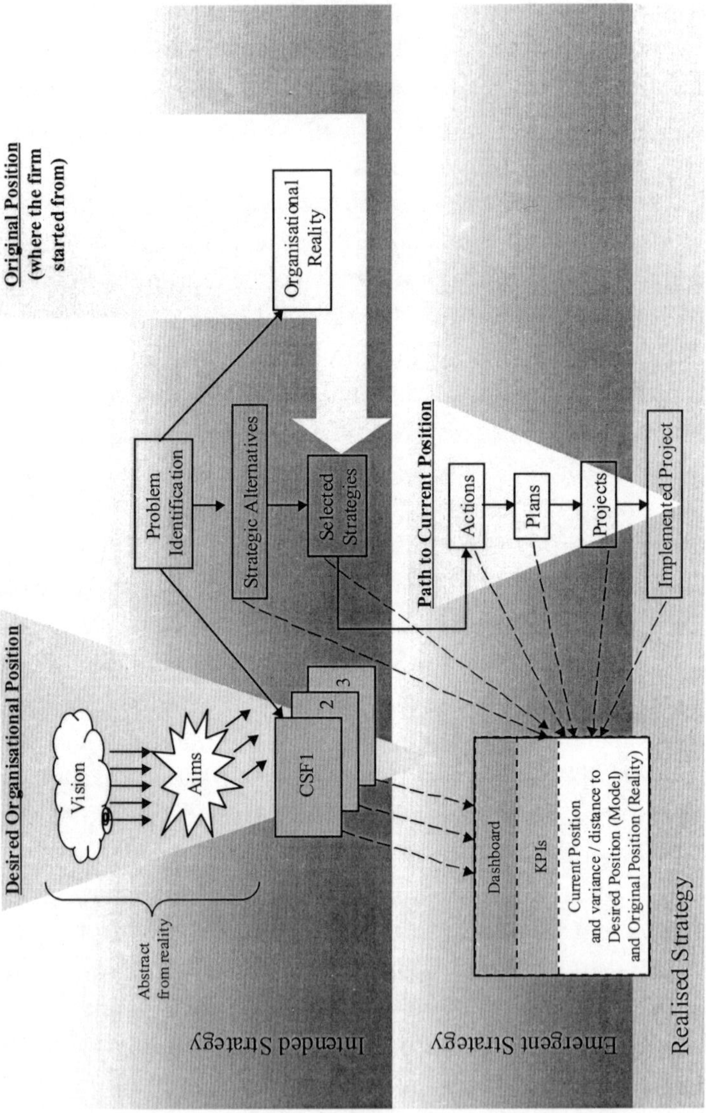

Adapted from Deasy, 1999

mented and, at the same time, is modified by their incremental contribution. It is worth noting that diagrams such as this one may fall in one of the traps identified by Langley *et al.* (1995) in their *Management Science* article on studying decision-making. In this article, they noted that there is a continuum in previous research from contributions that based their models of decision-making on rationality to contributions that emphasised the anarchic nature of managerial decision-making. On this continuum they highlighted how Cohen *et al.*'s (1972) garbage can model enabled researchers to put forward some explanations for the chaos that they observe in many organisations. They claimed, however, that such models can become a bit too convenient as

> whatever researchers fail to understand using more traditional theories can safely be dumped into the Garbage Can (p. 262).

By extension, we have remarked that diagrams such as the one in Figure 7.3 often feature arrows between components of the model without the research presenting any tangible data or analysis of what the relationship represented by the arrow consists of. Thus, such diagrams claim to explain far more than they actually explain and whatever is not understood properly can safely be represented by an arrow (i.e. dumped into the garbage can). This is a drawback of such diagrams, but it should not stop students from trying to extend existing models or developing their own insofar as contributions, such as that in Figure 7.3, are quite sufficient at the level of a master's thesis and have merit in themselves, even when they do not provide all the answers. It is quite acceptable to propose a framework and to let future researchers speculate or investigate the nature of the relationship between certain elements of the framework.

Students who reach that final stage can be satisfied to have put together a nice framework that was useful for their study and that they developed slowly but surely until it was robust enough to feature into their conclusion chapter. At the end of the whole research process, such diagrams come to represent and symbolise the research project itself and readers can identify the different elements that were at the core of the research and where they came from.

Chapter Eight

Writing Up: Some Comments About the Finished Product

Throughout the research project, students should seek very specific advice and guidance from their supervisors regarding what constitutes a suitable empirical target and what level of detail is required in terms of analysis and content. In a sense, therefore, the title of this chapter is slightly misleading in its term "writing up". By now students should have completed drafts of the major sections of the dissertation document. Supervisors should be able to state clearly and specifically what remains to be done in the final tidying up and what is the icing on the cake. Once such an agreement has been reached, both students and supervisors will be reassured by the knowledge that they have charted a path to the end of the research project. This will correspond to a period when students disappear from sight and spend all their time writing up, formatting tables and figures and creating nice styles for their headings.

The need to present regular drafts of the various sections of work to supervisors cannot be over-emphasised. This allows for the development of a style of writing and aids in reaching the level of detail to match what is required of the student by the degree programme or by department rules. Based on the time of the year, supervisors may be more or less busy or they might be on a holiday break. Some planning is therefore required so that students are able to receive feedback on their work-in-progress within a reasonable period of time; thus, students can aim at producing the full document in time for the deadline agreed with their supervisor. It is very important that students find out as early as possible what date they have to be ready for. There might be some additional tasks that must be performed before the thesis can be submitted, such as binding or producing a suitable bibliography, and these take a lot of time. One or two months before the final deadline, students and supervisors should put together a countdown to the finished product that takes all these additional tasks into account and students should endeavour to stick to this schedule.

The Beginning: The Introduction Chapter

While this chapter is the first to meet the reader of any dissertation, students should leave it to be the the last one written. For many students, this can be slightly confusing, and as such they are unsure as to what should be included here. This chapter will be relatively short and usually contains the following elements: an outline of the background to the research study, a statement of the research objective, research questions and research methodology and finally an outline of the chapters that make up the body of the dissertation.

The main difficulty in writing the introduction stems from a need to re-express that which may have already taken much work to put into one formulation acceptable to both student and supervisor. However, a little patience and thought should help resolve any difficulties. While a certain level of language and writing competency is expected of all postgraduate programmes, students should consider this chapter as a way to explain to someone not at all familiar with the research project exactly what it was all about.

The Middle

The middle chunk of the dissertation consists of the literature review chapter(s), the research methodology chapter and those chapters used in organising, presenting and analysing the data gathered. If students have presented these to their supervisors at regular intervals throughout the research process, then only very minor realignments will be required here. Students may have found additional supporting evidence justifying their research needs. For example, the results of the research process may have pointed to a differing research objective than that previously posited or a previously unthought of research question may have emerged from the study. This is not something to worry about, provided the student agrees all such changes with the supervisor and they do not involve significant redrafting of major sections of the work. However, the fact that such changes often occur during the research process means that a careful reading of the final draft must be undertaken by the researcher to verify the coherence and consistency of the presentation of the goals of the research and of its research questions. Key areas of a dissertation that must be checked for such problems include the first chapter, the conclusions of the literature review, the presentation of the research questions in the research methodology chapter, the headings and sub-headings of the findings chapter(s) and the final chapter of the dissertation where the objectives and findings of the research might be restated. These areas are the most obvious for such verification, but nothing will replace a cover to cover scrutiny by the researcher himself or herself.

The End

The final section in the main body of the completed dissertation is the presentation of findings and conclusions. This is perhaps one of the more difficult chapters to write; thus, many drafts may need to be submitted before the supervisor is happy. Students also feel compelled to include a long list of directions for future research in this section. The inclusion of such a task set is not really necessary and may be of little use to the reader (though it might be required in the context of specific masters programmes). A more constructive approach to this section is to point out, in as positive a manner as possible, any specific limitations which apply (or may be applied if the student fails to do so) to the findings of the study and what specific means could be taken to overcome these regarding future theoretical contributions. Students should note that the main readers of the study in its present dissertation format will be well aware of the limitations inherent in postgraduate research, particularly in regard to resources of time, experience and funding.

In writing this final chapter, students should take a realistic look at what they have achieved and concentrate on the most essential, most valid and most defendable aspects of their research results. Thus, choices might have to be made, but the research project will always seem more robust if the claims made in the conclusions are close to the research questions and streamlined and if lengthy catalogues of half-baked pseudo findings are avoided.

The Other Bits – From the Title Page Onwards

Be warned: putting together a final completed dissertation or thesis takes a lot longer than most students think and plan for. A completed bundle of chapters must then be wrapped into cover pages, an abstract, a table of contents, lists of figures and tables, a complete bibliography and appendices as needed and bound to the requirements of the student's college or university (the Exams office of your university should be able to provide such guidelines).

By now, the dissertation will need a title if it has not acquired one already. Care should be exercised in choosing the title. It needs to be informative regarding the subject matter and content of the dissertation, but, at the same time, it should not contain more than fifteen to twenty words, each of which uniquely contributes to conveying the overall contents of the document. Looking at titles previously used by students of your programme will be a useful guide.

The abstract is a short, concise summary of the dissertation. Usually of no more than one A4 page in length, the abstract condenses the contents of the dissertation. Students should ensure that they comply with any word limit placed upon the abstract by their individual institution. The abstract should contain a short summary of the research issue, a statement of the research objective and research questions, a brief description of the chosen research methodology used and an outline of the main findings and conclusions from the dissertation. It is different from the introduction chapter in that this simply provides the reader with 'signposts' of what is to come and how it is organised; the abstract is essentially a short summary of the completed research project with particular emphasis on the findings and conclusions.

The table of contents is compiled from the headings used in each of the chapters. Students will save much time and effort if they learn at an early stage how to generate automatic versions of this in the word processing package they use (e.g. alt + Insert + Index and Tables functions in Microsoft Word). If students opt to type in their table of contents, they need to remain vigilant in ensuring that all changes to page numbers are subsequently incorporated. It is also useful at this point to provide the reader with a list of the tables and figures that are to be found throughout the document.

The most important item at the end of the dissertation is the bibliography. This is basically an alphabetical listing of the references used in the dissertation. More specific guidelines regarding its construction are contained in the 'Practical Publishing: Frequently Asked Questions' section of Part Two. All appendices used must also be placed at the back of the document. These will usually contain additional information which, while not directly relevant to the dissertation itself, may give the reader further insight into the project if they feel they require it. Examples of materials to be found in appendices include schedules of site visits and interviews, sample copies of questionnaires or surveys used, lists of archival documentation accessed or background information on case study organisations.

Pitfalls and Potential Problems

Once students have reached this stage in the dissertation process, they are nearly there! A number of difficulties may still be encountered, but good advance planning will avoid many of these. Some of the most typical pitfalls and problems that may arise at this stage are outlined below.

- *Missing references:* from the outset, students should begin to construct their bibliography. This means beginning at the point at which the research topic was initially considered. One way of doing this in paper format is to purchase a standard address notebook from any stationary store; thus, you can automatically list each reference under the appropriate alphabetical identifier. Alternatively, an electronic listing can be maintained on an ongoing basis. This will save much time in the later stages. Any references not used can be deleted – this is much quicker than having to type all those you do use. See Part Two for information on constructing a bibliography. When references have gone missing, it can be very difficult to find them again. Often, students only have a name and a year of publication to go on and they must rely on the memory and knowledge of the staff of the department. This may work for mainstream references such as Patton (1990) or Miles and Huberman (1994), but may turn into a big time-waster in the case of more obscure or more specialised references. In fact, once students have been made aware of the problem, there is really no excuse for them to "lose" references they have used in their research.

- *Time:* students often don't allow time in their planning for activities such as proof-reading, printing and binding. When one is reaching the end of the research process, it can be an immense help to locate a trusted proof-reader who has not had much previous contact with the materials. Thus, they will spot any inconsistencies, as well as spelling and grammar mistakes. Printing and binding the finished document also takes time. Students should ascertain the specific requirements of their institution well in advance and know exactly how they will go about these tasks.

- *Consistency:* the entire thesis document must read as one complete publication and not as a disconnected series of chapters (even though each element does represent a distinct aspect or phase in the research project). Quite often, all that is needed to achieve this is the insertion of cross-referencing in some of the key connecting paragraphs. A clear, concise introduction chapter also helps in this regard.

PART TWO

COPING WITH PANDORA'S BOX

PART TWO

COPING WITH PANDORA'S BOX

The use of the reference to Pandora's Box for this part of the book deserves some specific comments. When we were deciding what the structure of the book should be, we discovered that there were many aspects of research work that needed to be included, but that were difficult to integrate into a coherent whole. After scratching our heads for a long time, we realised that this lack of structure was characteristic of the research process and we decided not to attempt to force these important elements into an artificial structure. This is how we arrived at the reference to Pandora's Box, a mysterious and limitless array of things that researchers must be able to cope with and know about before they start, and which can make or break a research dissertation.

One feature of the Box, of course, is that once it has been opened, countless rules of thumb, things to do, improvements, alternative sources of information and strange words will come pouring out in overwhelming fashion. Part Two of the book is therefore presented in a number of separate sections that come to play an important part at specific points in the process described in Part One. As such, it does not seem important to read them prior to undertaking the research, but they take on particular importance when their time has come. Part Two can therefore be used as a reference manual for specific aspects of the research process on a need-to-use basis. It includes information on the following items:

- Presenting the research proposal.

- Do's and Don'ts: The Ten Commandments and the Seven Deadly Sins of writing dissertations.

- Use of the Internet and other computer-based sources for searching material.

- List of web sites.

- List of journals in the business area.

- Research methods: a brief look at some of the main research tools available to postgraduate researchers.

- Practical publishing: frequently asked questions.

- Glossary: key ideas that shaped research.

- Relevant bibliography: signposts to further readings.

- Template for non-disclosure agreement; introductory letter to present your research to potential informants.

- Dissertation management checklist: mapping the book to the practical experience (your personal odyssey).

Presenting the Research Proposal: Some Guidelines

Formal presentations of materials at the proposal stage are a vital element of many postgraduate programmes. Some guidelines on how to prepare for such reviews are presented here. The points made are equally valid in relation to presentations of literature review materials, progress reports or of the finished research product.

Consider the objective of the presentation: you are putting forward for comment the topic you have chosen and anticipate spending the next months working on. Thus, you must accomplish a number of things: the audience needs to be quite clear on the subject area and within that what specific sub-set of it your topic encompasses and what it does not include. This means that any ambiguous phrases or titles open to more than one interpretation must clearly be defined within the context of how you are going to use them. The first part of the presentation will involve a brief review of existing research in that subject area and topic, and should seek to give the audience answers to three specific questions:

1. What is the extent of current research in the subject area/research topic? Who said so?

2. Is that subject area/research topic worthy of further research?

3. Where does your chosen research project fit into the answers to the first two questions above?

At this point, it is worth pointing out that you will not be expected to have comprehensive answers to each of these questions, but you will need to demonstrate that you have given some thought to them and are interested in the research topic. The purpose of the presentation is partly one of guiding you, the student, towards the most efficient means of structuring your proposed course of research and this may include forcing you to reconsider some of the initial aspects of your plan.

The second part of the proposal presentation involves giving the audience some sense of how you intend to operationalise your research project. Once again, your proposal need not be cast in stone, but may, for example, provide two possible means of 'doing' the research bit. The final choice will obviously be made at a later stage in the process. Alternatively, you may propose a number of possible organisations, the final choice to be made based on ease of access. At the level of a master's thesis or dissertation, such trade-offs are generally quite acceptable. At the end of the presentation, you need to leave the audience with some sort of conclusion. The easiest way to do this is to restate briefly what your research need is, the research objective and possible research directions you see as fulfilling that need, and the chosen means by which you intend to gather and analyse the data. In summary:

- Slides greatly facilitate the delivery of presentations; do not, however, attempt to put too much detail onto the slides or else the audience will spend more time reading the slides than listening to you! Use about three or four slides in total.

- If you are given a time limit for the presentation, stick to it.

- Practice your presentation beforehand, and if possible, use the technology you intend to use during the presentation. You will become more used to hearing the sound of your own voice and you will know in advance that the technology works.

- Take note (i.e. written notes!) of any suggestions, comments, etc. made to you during the course of the presentation or in any discussion time at the end. They may not seem relevant now, but could suddenly become very clear at a later date when you may not be able to access the person who made them. This applies particularly to interesting references that may be provided to you by others.

Do's and Don'ts: The Ten Commandments of Thesis Writing!

1. *Do* pick a topic that you feel strongly about. It is no use chasing something half-heartedly only to find out that one has no interest in it after a few weeks or months. Writing a dissertation takes a long time – it might as well be enjoyable.

2. *Do not* pick a topic that it is so novel that no one has researched it before you. It may not be researchable at all or at the very least you will not find any convincing literature to help you. Make sure (in discussions with your supervisor) that there is ample material to quote from. Your task will be considerably simplified.

3. *Do not* expect your supervisor to immediately read material you submit. Supervisors have a hard time too and they go through periods where they have enormous quantities of work that must be taken care of (such as examination corrections). Plan with them when you are going to submit large portions of the work and when you can expect feedback. It will also help if you don't submit low-grade work full of typing errors and so badly presented that the supervisor has difficulty concentrating on the content of the work.

4. *Do* respect the deadlines you set with your supervisor (unless something serious comes up). Not sticking to deadlines rapidly puts you on a slippery slope that can lead to additional years, loss of commitment and motivation, loss of attention from your supervisor and never finishing. Remember that the best dissertation is the finished one and that there is nothing wrong with obtaining results fast.

5. *Do* behave ethically and responsibly in your approach to fieldwork. The penalty can be very high for students who invent empirical data (such as interviews, case data, etc.) or misrepresent

what was said to them by informants. The penalty can even be far higher for students who breach confidentiality agreements (verbal or otherwise) or whose actions result in complaints from industry actors. Many universities will not hesitate to expel students from their programmes in the face of such misconduct and, by and large, it is a totally fitting punishment.

6. *Do not* leave it until the last minute to chase your references. However tedious the task of keeping track of your references is, it is an absolute requirement that you should know where articles or chapters appeared and that you kept track of the page number of your citations. The time spent in chasing a reference or a page number at the end of the process is approximately ten times the time it takes to record it properly first time when the article or the book is in your hands.

7. *Do not* try to do too much. Focus on a small number of well-defined research questions. A major difference between good and bad dissertations is the extent to which students manage to tie down what their research is about with some certainty. Especially in case study research, it is paramount to understand what one's study is about before the vagueness of the questions asked leads to unmanageable amounts of data or to a vacuum of definite findings.

8. *Do* ensure that the dissertation you present is consistent in terms of its aims and findings. The final stage in the work is to read through the full draft document to verify that wherever goals are stated they are the same throughout, that wherever the research questions are stated they are strictly the same, that whenever findings are stated they are the same and do not materialise out of thin air in the conclusion chapter (if there is one) without being from empirical data earlier.

9. *Do* leave ample time at the end to edit your dissertation to high standards. There is little excuse for working hard for several

months on a research project only to submit a slapdash report about it. You will need at least two weeks to make the document, its tables and figures and its appendices as nice as they deserve to be. You also need to build in some time for printing and binding the document if you are not doing it yourself. It will also be a great help if you can line up a few proof-readers (your supervisor cannot be expected to play this role) to eliminate as many typos and grammatical mistakes as possible (the spellchecker can only do so much).

10. *Do not* start a new job before the thesis is finished (unless absolutely snookered into doing so). It is a fallacy to think that one might ever finish a thesis after starting a new job. The demands placed on you over the initial twelve months of employment will rule out any chance of you spending the required time on your research work. Even getting an agreement from your employer may not be sufficient for you to find the time required. If the new employer wants you badly enough, they will understand that you need a few more weeks to finish. Beyond this, it is your call to decide whether the thesis you have started is not important enough to hold you back.

'Seven Deadly Sins': The Researcher's Downfall!

1. *Statistics:* students can fall foul of the ease with which huge numbers of variables can easily be coded and 'crunched' through statistical packages, resulting in the proof of extremely meaningless sets of relationships. Data collection and generation using statistical means/tools represents just one step in the research process; the real skill of the researcher lies in the intelligent and constructive interpretation of those findings.

2. *Plagiarism:* your dissertation is meant to be an original work, and while imitation may be the most sincere form of flattery, your supervisor may have read the 'original' materials you present before, in particular if (s)he was the one who wrote them in the first place! At the very least, a supervisor will notice the changes in writing style.

3. *Presentation:* poor presentation, spelling and grammar are inexcusable in an era of widespread word processor availability in third-level institutions. Your supervisor should not be expected to serve as proof-reader and spell-checker, and indeed will become very annoyed if valuable time (both theirs and yours) is wasted is so doing.

4. *Deadlines:* you yourself are ultimately responsible for the completion of your dissertation. Do not expect your supervisor to waste his or her time chasing you looking for drafts of chapters. If you decide to do nothing and then wonder why you are watching an honours grade slowly disappear, please remember who had the benefit of the time spent not working on a dissertation.

5. *Technology:* the time to check that your tape recorder is working is in the office or postgrad room the day before you embark upon interviews/field research. One of the most common 'excuse' themes presented to supervisors to explain relative lack of progress by students is that of 'technological failure'. Under this heading is also included the need to maintain adequate back-up copies of your work and to save working documents at regular intervals (i.e. at least every 30 minutes). Remember to keep the pause button on your tape recorder off!

6. *Referencing:* no matter how many times they are told, there are always students who fail to keep good records in relation to references found. It is not enough to refer to 'that page in the middle with someone like maybe John Browne or . . .'. Chasing references is one of the most frustrating exercises for students and supervisors alike, particularly if your supervisor has pointed out the absence of that reference on more than one occasion and you have yet to heed his or her advice.

7. *Creativity:* possibly the worst of all misdemeanours, creativity as used here refers to the deliberate misinterpretation of research findings, the drafting of fictional research data or any other such unethical activity. Field research and survey methodology strategies are typical areas open to the creativity of less diligent students, who are better advised to note that even if their research turns up nothing they consider to be noteworthy, their supervisor may not be of the same opinion. In many instances, finding nothing can actually be a finding in itself if the correct research questions are asked.

Use of the Internet and other Computer-based Sources for Searching Material

While the Internet has been with us for quite a long time (in fact, since 1969), it has only become the worldwide communication medium it now is since around 1992. The development of the World Wide Web and the far more attractive interface it allows have drawn the very large investments that were required for the Internet's fast growth. These investments have resulted in a much better infrastructure (giving faster access times and allowing far greater traffic), better software to navigate and retrieve information, far more potential sites from which to get information and, of course, much easier access to the Internet from home, work or from the many workstations that universities make available to their students.

From the point of view of the researcher, the Internet is primarily a communication medium through the use of electronic mail. E-mail enables researchers who do not have the opportunity or the money to get together on a regular basis to correspond and even collaborate to produce research that has broader relevance or that crosses cultural boundaries. The Internet has also become the fastest way to obtain articles that have been published a long time ago or that appeared in non-mainstream publications, such as smaller conferences or working papers from small business schools. Most recent papers bear the mail address of their authors who are, by and large, keen to disseminate their work (even to 'mere' postgraduate researchers!). We are aware of a number of instances in which students writing simple essays on a given topic have sent e-mails to high calibre, renowned professors in that topic field and have received long messages within a few days. In another instance, an author contacted about one of their old working papers responded with more recent and more relevant papers.

In cases where the mail address of a particular researcher may not be known, a simple search for their name in a search engine such as Altavista (www.digital.altavista.com) may be sufficient to access a web page that features their address or, even better, their personal homepage. Alternatively, students may try to locate the department or the school from which a researcher operates and get in touch with the librarian or site manager for more information (a mail address is always readily available on the homepage of a site).

Finally, the Internet can be used to directly locate material of relevance to the study. However, such direct searching may not yield very good results. Much time can be spent on trying to locate articles on specific, narrow topics, such as 'executive information systems', without any convincing article being identified. The fact that the Internet can become a time-waster rather than a time-saver requires that its resources be used with discernment. For mainstream topics, such as 'the balanced scorecard', 'decision support systems' or 'the work of managers', it is unwise to use the Internet directly. Such topics are well-bounded and have already been extensively researched. There is little rationale for a direct search on the Internet for these topics insofar as many sources of information are available. Academic staff can be found in most institutions who are knowledgeable on these topics and who can point to a dozen key articles from which more can be obtained by association. When such key articles can be found, the Internet might be more usefully employed to get in contact with researchers who are active in the area and may be willing to answer questions and suggest further readings.

A colleague from a German university reported a funny story that illustrates how searching the Internet can be a futile exercise. He told us how he had instructed students to write an essay on the development of executive systems (as opposed to the development of more simple information systems). After two weeks his students came back to him and complained that the topic was far too difficult: no material could be located anywhere. The lecturer was amazed that such difficulties should have arisen and asked the students where they had been looking for material. They explained how several of them had spent a number of days on the Internet and had failed to come up with one single relevant paper! He then asked them how much time they had spent in the library . . . only to discover that they had not even tried there!

List of Web Sources

General Search Engines/Directories

- **The Electronic Library:** www.elibrary.com

  Search for articles in popular sources (mostly magazines, book reviews etc.), but nevertheless good for current material.

- **Yahoo:** www.yahoo.com

  Not very useful for scientific data, but better for general searches such as planning a holiday to recover after completing the dissertation.

- **Yahoo:** www.yahoo.co.uk

  Limits your browsing effectively when looking for materials of Irish or British interest.

- **Webcrawler:** www.web.crawler.com

  Allows thematic searches of the Web, including a people finder.

- **Magellan:** www.mckinley.com

  Another thematic guide which features predefined categories (business, travels etc.).

- **Infoseek:** guide.infoseek.com (www.go.com)

  Allows for complex search strings in a number of predefined categories, such as business, money etc. The company-search and follow-an-industry facilities provide interesting opportunities to identify potential case studies.

- **Lycos Inc.:** www.lycos.co.uk

  This is the search engine maintained by Carnegie Mellon University. It is similar to the others and enables searches in specific categories.

- **Excite:** www.excite.com

  A web site more dedicated to scientific information but also news-oriented.

- **AltaVista:** www.altavista.com

Provides good facilities for advanced searching.

- **HotBot:** www.hotbot.lycos.com

Offers an impressive range of possibilities for specifying your search; use the options for limiting your search carefully to avoid unintentionally excluding relevant data.

Sites more focused on Research

- **HytelNet:** www.cam.ac.uk

This is the web site of the University of Cambridge. It presents a very complete listing of online catalogues, archival sites, linkages to databases, bibliographies (from the World Bank to the US government publications site), bulletin boards, etc. It gives access to so much relevant information that it is possible to get lost in it for a few hours.

- **Institute for Scientific Information:** wos.heanet.ie

This site presents an effective search engine to locate references in the areas of social sciences, art and humanities and general science. Indexes can also be searched by name of the author, by topic or by place of publication.

- **Publishers' home pages:** www.lights.com/publisher

Listings of most publishing houses classified per geographical area. Also features search engine for any book you might be looking for.

- **Social Sciences Information Gateway (SOSIG):** sosig.ac.uk

- **Previous Theses:** www.theses.com

An index to theses accepted for higher degrees by the Universities of Great Britain and Ireland.

- **Company Annual Reports Online (CAROL):** www.carol.co.uk

Official Publications/Professional Institutions

- **Irish Government Departments:** www.irlgov.ie

  Irish government site with links to other Irish organisations and agencies.

- **Central Statistics Office:** www.cso.ie

  Also has links to European Member Official Statistical Bodies.

- **Chartered Institute of Management Accountants (CIMA):** www.cima.org.uk

- **Institute of Chartered Accountants in Ireland (ICAI):** www.icai.ie

- **Association of Chartered Certified Accountants (ACCA):** www.acca.co.uk

- **Guide to Statistics on the Web:** http://www.execpc.com/~lelberg/statistics.html

- **Wall Street Journal:** http://wsj.com.tour.html

- **US Stock Quotes and Financial Information:** http://quote.yahoo.com

- **UK Accounting Resources:** http://sosig.esrc.bris.ac.uk/subjects/UK/account.html

- **Anet: Austrialian Academic Network:** http://www.csu.edu.au/anet/

- **ISWorld – The Site of the ISWORLD Network:** http://www.isworld.org/isworld/

To Locate an Individual Using the Internet

The following can be worth a try if you are trying to find a contact e-mail address:

- **Bigfoot:** www.bigfoot.com

- **Four11:** www.four11.com

- **IAF (Intranet Address Finder):** www.iaf.net

- **Switchboard:** www.switchboard.com

- **WhoWhere?:** www.whowhere.com

Note that this list and the addresses provided were correct at the time this book went to press. It is, however, unavoidable that some of these will change over the months and years.

List of Journals in the Business Area

The lists presented below constitute a sample of the most used journals in accounting, management, IS and related areas. It cannot claim to be exhaustive because the number of publications on paper or electronically has grown and is growing at such a rate that such lists would have to be updated all the time. Thus, the journals included below are the most common sources of references to existing research and students should consider them as potentially useful, depending upon the area they are researching (journal titles are normally a good indication of the topics covered, though some journals are more specialised than others).

The way to use this listing is to search for the names of relevant journals on the Internet so as to find their home page or in the catalogue of your library. When you have found the shelving area where the journals are stored, you should take them to a quiet area of the library and read through all available back issues for any article likely to give you good ideas. Then, select the most useful articles and photocopy them to integrate them into your work (periodicals normally cannot be taken out so you must make copies of whatever you are going to use in your research). Do not forget to replace the material where you found it: libraries are difficult to keep in order and every little bit helps.

In some institutions, journals such as the ones in the list below are classified according to the quality of the research they present. However useful such classifications can be in some instances (such as for potential authors to know what publications are going to be most regarded by their peers), it may be of little relevance to students writing master's dissertations. All the journals included in the list below are 'academic' enough and they can be used without worrying about whether they are suitable sources. In any case, as authors of this book we are not going to be dragged into a spurious debate as to whether journal A is intrinsically better than journal B and we have presented the names below in alphabetical order.

- *Accountancy*
- *Accounting and Business Research*
- *Accounting, Auditing and Accountability Journal*
- *Accounting History*
- *Accounting Horizons*
- *Accounting, Management and Information Technologies (AMIT)*
- *Accounting, Organisations and Society*
- *Accounting Review*
- *ACM Computing Surveys*
- *ACM Transactions on Computer Human Interaction*
- *ACM Transactions on Information Systems*
- *Acta Informatica*
- *Administrative Science Quarterly*
- *Artificial Intelligence*
- *Australian Journal of Information Systems*
- *Berkeley Technology Law Journal*
- *British Accounting Review*
- *British Management Review*
- *California Management Review*
- *Communications of the ACM (CACM)*
- *Contemporary Accounting Research*
- *Critical Perspectives on Accounting*
- *DataBase*
- *Decision Sciences Journal*
- *Decision Support Systems*
- *Economics, Business and Management Science*
- *European Accounting Review*

- *European Journal of Information Systems (EJIS)*
- *European Journal of Operational Research (EJOR)*
- *First Monday: Peer Reviewed Journal on the Internet about the Internet*
- *Harvard Business Review (HBR)*
- *IBM Systems Journal*
- *IEEE Transactions / Journals*
- *Information and Management*
- *Information Society Journal*
- *Information Strategy*
- *Information Systems Journal*
- *Information Systems Research*
- *Information Technology and People*
- *International Journal of Information Management*
- *Irish Accounting Review*
- *Journal of Accounting and Economics (JAE)*
- *Journal of Accounting Literature (JAL)*
- *Journal of Accounting Research (JAR)*
- *Journal of Business*
- *Journal of Cost Management*
- *Journal of Decision Systems*
- *Journal of Financial Information Systems*
- *Journal of Information Technology (JIT)*
- *Journal of Information Technology Management (JIM)*
- *Journal of Management*
- *Journal of Management Accounting Research (JMAR)*
- *Journal of Management Information Systems (JIMS)*
- *Journal of Organizational Computing and Electronic Commerce*
- *Journal of Strategic Change*

- *Journal of Strategic Information Systems (JSIS)*
- *Journal of Systems Management*
- *Long Range Planning*
- *Management Accounting (CIMA journal)*
- *Management Information Systems Quarterly*
- *Management Science*
- *Scandinavian Journal of Information Systems*
- *Scandinavian Journal of Management*
- *SIAM Journal on Computing*
- *SIS-EJOURNAL: The Electronic Journal of Strategic Information Systems*
- *Sloan Management Review*
- *Strategic Management Journal*

Other sources

- *CIMA occasional papers series*
- *CIMA research reports*
- *Executive Systems Research Centre Research and Discussion Papers*

Research Methods: A Brief Look

This section of Pandora's Box is concerned with some of the more dominant research methods available for postgraduate research in the business area. A brief definition of each method is provided, along with the main advantages and disadvantages each offers as part of a research approach. This section is not intended to be all-inclusive in any sense, but rather, should serve as a starting point along the road towards building and defining one's own research approach. Thus, each of the methods dealt with are considered more on an individual basis than in relation to each other. Such cross-method comparisons and evaluations are left to each individual student, as this is a task most effectively accomplished within the specific frame of reference of an individual's research objective and research questions.

Field Research

A style of investigation traditionally associated with the social sciences and anthropology, field research essentially offers an insider view from an outsider's perspective (Burgess, 1982). Following from Yin[1], field research can be defined as

> an empirical investigation that investigates a contemporary phenomenon within its real life context; when the boundaries between the phenomenon and context are not clearly evident; and in which multiple sources of evidence are used (Yin, 1989; p. 23).

Advantages:

- Depicts the research topic in its natural context.

- Allows for a sense of the evolution of processes over time and for the emergence of new practices.

- Very rich data gathering, involving the use of many methods and data sources.

- Very effective in situations where the theoretical foundations available are meagre or do not enable the a priori formulation of research issues.

---

[1] Yin uses the term 'case studies' but is essentially referring to field research.

Disadvantages:

- Involves more than one research method, and therefore research instruments used need very careful consideration.

- Time-consuming, especially if key informants are difficult to locate.

- Site selection and access may be problematic.

- Whilst the findings generated are very realistic in the context of the case studied, the researcher must sacrifice the generalisability of results to the focus on a single or small number of instances of the phenomenon under study.

- Individual researchers can place different interpretations on the same data.

Administrative Records and Other Documents

Most activities leave an extensive audit trail within an organisation that can be used to corroborate and augment other data sources. To cite Bruns (1989),

> Identifiable professionals use documented processes to process information, records and reports with established distribution lists. In many situations, producers and users are easily linked to each other and are available at a single location (p. 163).

Advantages:

- Means of triangulation.

- Does not require active participation on the part of organisational actors.

Disadvantages:

- May be difficulties with access, particularly regarding confidential or sensitive materials.

Interviews

There are many different types of interviews, ranging from structured, whereby the interviewee is asked a set of predefined questions which he/she may or may not have been given in advance, through to unstructured interviews, which more resemble a conversation.

Advantages:

- Allows the researcher a very rich means of collecting data from key informants.
- Unstructured interviews greatly facilitate the start-up phase of the data gathering function.
- Structured interviews allow the researcher the advantages of a survey while minimising many of the disadvantages.
- Areas of interest can be explored in greater detail than possible using other methods.

Disadvantages:

- Locating key informants may be problematic.
- If taped, much additional work must be done to transcribe those tapes.

Observation

This has been the root source of all human knowledge and can become a tool of scientific enquiry to the extent that it is systematically planned, recorded and related to the research question and subjected to checks and controls for reliability and validity (Sellitz *et al.*, 1967).

Advantages:

- Less demanding of active participation on the part of the entity under study.
- Offers the possibility of recording behaviour as it actually and normally occurs.

Disadvantage:

- Researchers need to be aware of the Hawthorne Effect: individuals may show changes in behaviour patterns once they have an awareness of being observed.

Surveys

Surveys remain one of the most accessible means of acquiring large volumes of empirical data. Once robust questionnaires have been designed and a suitable sample has been identified, data should start flowing in and desciption and analysis are comparatively easy.

Advantages:

- Allows the researcher to focus on a small number of parameters specifically relevant to the study.

- If well designed, surveys should serve the researcher equally well in the organisation and analysis of the data gathered.

- Allows for large sample size.

- Tends to deal with phenomenon already 'institutionalised' in organisations.

Disadvantages:

- The realism of the research result is sacrificed to the focus on many cases but few variables.

- To an extent, the respondents will be self-selecting, and the researcher has little effective control in this regard.

- Gives little insight into the causes behind the phenomenon being studied.

Practical Publishing: Frequently Asked Questions

What is a Bibliography?
A bibliography is an alphabetical listing of books, journal articles, web pages and any other source materials used in the writing of a dissertation. Specifically not included here are field data sources of information, such as internal company publications, copies of published accounts, minutes of meetings, etc. Students should list these items separately as sources of evidence. Particular programmes may require specific formats (including fonts) in the construction of the bibliography; if this is not the case for you, then use 'consistency' as an over-riding guide. Brennan (1998) lists the following as details to record in respect of references:

- Book: Author(s) surname, initials; Year of publication; Title of book; Place of publication; Publisher.

  Example: Patton, M. (1990), *Qualitative evaluation and research methods*, Sage Publications, Newbury Park, CA.

- Article in book: Author(s) surname, initials; Year of publication; "Title of article"; Title of book; Editor(s) surname, initials; Title of Book; Place of publication; Publisher; Page numbers of the article.

  Example: Kulka, R.A. (1982), Idiosyncrasy and circumstance: choices and constraints in the research process in McGrath, Martin and Kulka (ed.), *Judgement Calls in Research*, Sage Publication, Beverly Hills, pp. 41-69.

- Article: Author(s) surname, initials; Year of publication; Title of journal; Title of journal; Volume and issue number; Page numbers.

  Example: Kaplan, B. and Duchon, D. (1988), Combining qualitative and quantitative methods in information systems research: a case study, *Management Informations Systems Quarterly*, 12(4), 571-586.

How do I Make Reference to other Articles/Books/Web Pages?

There are two general types of reference to previous works: direct quotation and argument support. A direct quotation arises where you use the text of another exactly as it is written. It is important to make sure you transcribe the sentences correctly, place the quote within the context the original author had intended[2] and provide a detailed reference back to the original material. An example is as follows:

> Re-engineering, like democracy, religion and marriage, is theoretically a sensible concept. But like every good idea promoted as a solution to all ills that ail, it has the potential to serve the opposite purpose (Strassman, 1994; p. 119).

The complete reference to the original Strassmann text should be included in the bibliography section of the dissertation.

A more complicated form of direct quotation is that in which the text of the quote is taken as a pre-existing quotation in another piece of work. Consider the following example: Burgess (1982) cited the work of Schatzman and Strauss (1973). If you now wish to use the same quotation from Schatzman and Strauss (1973) but have taken it from the Burgess (1982) text, then the format is as follows:

> Field method is not an exclusive method in the same sense say that experimentation is. Field method is more like an umbrella of activity beneath which any technique may be used for gaining the desired information, and for processes of thinking about this information (Schatzman and Strauss, 1973; p. 14, cited in Burgess, 1982).

The complete reference to the Burgess text should be included in the bibliography section of the dissertation.

Where the work of others is used to **support** an argument or particular train of thought (you will have already seen numerous examples of this throughout the first section of this book) cite the authors' name(s) and the date of the publication. For example:

---

[2] The importance of this phrase cannot be over-stated. For example, take this citation from Strassmann (1994): students using only the first sentence completely misstate the intentions of the author by simply citing: "Re-engineering, like democracy, religion and marriage, is theoretically a sensible concept". The second sentence is needed to convey exactly what Strassmann's sentiments on the topic are.

> The important question is not how scientific the research
> design is, but how it serves to generate the level of proof
> wanted in the research and to reflect the state of existing
> knowledge in the research area (Miller, 1991).

Once again, the complete reference for Miller (1991) should be
included in the bibliography section.

References to web pages are a relatively new phenomenon is
research dissertations. It is clearer for the reader to compile a separate listing of web sources as an additional element to your bibliography. Web addresses are also relatively lengthy, therefore it is
better to use a summarised version in the body of the dissertation -
just make sure that the reader can easily equate this to the full reference in the bibliographic section.

Example: The following refers to the web pages of University
College Cork:

> The Department of Accounting, Finance and Information
> Systems has nineteen full-time staff, with research interests
> in managerial accounting, corporate finance and business
> information systems (w-UCC1)

Extract from bibliography:

w-UCC1:   http://www.ucc.ie/acad/afis.html

How do I Deal with More than one Author?

If there are only two authors, use both names, e.g. Smith and Jones
(1999). If there are more than two, then the phrase '*et al.*', literally
meaning '*and others*', can be used when referencing the work in
the text of the dissertation. However, the full listing of names should
be provided in the bibliography. Take, for example, Smith, Jones,
Murphy and Browne writing in 1998:

- In the text of the dissertation: (Smith *et al.*, 1998).

- In the bibliography: Smith, A., Jones, B., Murphy, C., and
  Browne, D., ...

General Rules for Presentation

One of the leading sources of guidelines for presentation of thesis and other research documents is the American Psychological Association (APA), which regularly publishes its Publication Manual. A number of web sites can give you access to these guidelines, such as:

- www.psychwww.com/resource/apacrib

- http://juno.concordia.ca/services/citations

However, in some respects these guidelines are very rigid and may not be totally required for master's students. Other web sites provide writing tips for students, including:

- http://www.columbia.edu/cu/ssw/write/electrnc

From a practical point of view, however, the following guidelines may be sufficient for most students:

- Check the page set-up in your word processor. Make sure it is set on A4 and that you have a margin of at least 2.5 cm (1 inch) all around. If the document is going to be sizeable, you might want to add a binding offset, i.e. an additional margin on the left-hand side which will facilitate reading your document once it is bound.

- Use consistent styles for your paragraphs, headings and sub-headings and your titles and legends. Set them once and for all in your word processor so you can then use them consistently from the early stages of your research. For instance, your quotes should always look the same, as is shown below:

  > A nice margin on the right-hand side and maybe a smaller one on the left-hand side. A different font or font size also looks nice. You can use italics to report things that were said in interviews, thereby differentiating literature from empirical evidence.

- Try not to insert blank lines between paragraphs. It is much neater to have a style that automatically adds six points before and after paragraph marks (e.g. look in Format Paragraph in MS Word).

- Try to avoid orphan lines at the top and bottom of your pages. You can prevent those by asking your software to remove orphans. This can prove troublesome with the flow of the text in some cases when you are trying to keep a legend stuck to a table or figure, but it makes for much nicer documents overall.

- Stick to the third person voice at all times. If you have to talk about something you have done or about choices you had to make, talk about the researcher and his (or her) study.

- Avoid displaying obvious gender bias such as, "as the manager . . . he will be involved in decision-making", unless you are making reference to a particular interviewee who happened to be male. In most cases, it is not too difficult to side step the problems by using plurals or using neutral statements.

- Avoid using light-hearted expressions or oral grammar, such as, "the manager could get involved in as many as, say, twenty decision per day" and never use slang, unless reporting on something that was volunteered by one of your interviewees (and even then, use some restraint if you judge that words that were used cannot be repeated).

- Try to balance the size of your paragraph and your sections. Avoid one-sentence paragraphs or one-sentence sections. If you have sentences on their own, read what is before and after to establish where they belong. If you have very short sections, ask yourself if they really form a new section.

- Try to remember what they told you about punctuation in school. A few well-placed commas do make an enormous difference to your sentences and how understandable they are. It is far more efficient to do this from day one rather than wait until the end and be told by your supervisor, "Oh, by the way, you must rewrite all that stuff. It isn't really very well-written at this stage. See if can you sort it out a bit better." It could take you a few days to sort it out a 'bit' better!

Glossary: A Quick Guide to the Important Ideas that have Shaped Research

- *A Posteriori:* a statement whose truth or not is determined based on experience of the events or context to which it relates, e.g. "The door is open".

- *A Priori:* a statement that holds true or false on its own merits, independent of experience, e.g. "2 + 3 = 5".

- *Action research* (see also participative research): a form of research strategy that allows the researcher to take part in the research itself through ongoing personal active involvement with the research field and the process of action and change taking place therein.

- *Construct validity:* see research validity / theoretical validity.

- *Deduction:* this approach uses "general results to ascribe properties to specific instances. An argument is held valid if it is impossible for the conclusions to be false if the premises are true" (Fitzgerald and Howcroft, 1997, p. 9).

- *Eclecticism:* matching the research method with the research question (Gable, 1994).

- *Empiricism:* leads to the idea that all science, both natural and social, should be free from beliefs and ideologies which cannot be justified in terms of the evidence presented, and has led to the development of positivism.

- *External validity:* the extent to which research findings can be generalised from the specific research context to more general statements.

- *Hermeneutics:* an approach to data analysis that emphasises how prior understandings and prejudices shape the interpretation of that data (Denzin and Lincoln, 1994).

- *Induction:* a process of theory development whereby "specific instances are used to arrive at overall generalisations, which can be expected, on the balance of probability. New evidence may cause conclusions to be revised" (Fitzgerald and Howcroft, 1997, p. 9).

- *Interpretivism:* no universal truth exists; analysis and understanding is rooted in the researcher's own individual frame of reference and in the context of the research, and thus cannot be neutral and independent of the research entity.

- *Paradigm:* the word paradigm can be defined as "an example serving as a model" (Webster's College Dictionary, Random House, 1990, p. 980) and has its roots in Latin grammatical construction. In a business context, a paradigm means the conventional wisdom or set of beliefs of how things arc done.

- *Participative research:* see action research.

- *Phenomenology:* concerns the search for the essence in a phenomenon, essence being that which gives the phenomenon its separate identity. Essence is not a physical attribute, however. For example, consider the topic "The success of Manchester United" – 'success' gives Man. United an identity as a 'successful' soccer club, and enables the study of "what makes Man. United successful". However, to operationalise the study requires initial consideration of 'success' and what it is.

- *Pluralism:* no single universally valid model of research exists (Gable, 1994).

- *Positivism:* concerned with the external reality, sometimes to the exclusion of concern with the process of observation itself. To be contrasted with phenomenology, which places primary concern on the observation, sometimes to the exclusion of concern for external validity. Positivism asserts that objective accounts of the world can be given independent of the researcher's appreciation of them. Knowledge is simply that accepted by society at a given time; thus "post-positivism is more a belief about knowledge, it is not a particular school of thought with any agreed set of propositions or tenets" (Hirschheim, 1985, p. 33). See also post-positivism.

- *Post-positivism:* see also positivism. Refers to the movement away from positivism as the only scientific research method, particularly in the social sciences. Proponents of post-positivism argue that reality can never be fully accounted for, only approximated.

- *Qualitative research:* refers to means of research from which the evidence from the data gathering function is primarily of a non-numeric nature per se.

- *Quantitative research:* involves the use of mathematical or statistical research methods to establish causal relationships.

- *Rationalism:* this is an argument that true knowledge can only be obtained through the use of reason and emphases the power of logic and mathematics in the search for the 'truth'.

- *Realism:* belief that "the external world consists of pre-existing hard, tangible structures which exist independently of an individual's cognition" (Fitzgerald and Howcroft, 1997, p. 9).

- *Research methodology:* this refers to the overall approach, and within that, the individual research methods and tools used to meet a given research objective. A clear and unambiguous statement of the research objective is therefore necessary to enable the selection of an appropriate research methodology and data collection techniques.

- *Research validity:* validity concerns the quality of fit between an observation and the basis on which that observation has been made. In more specific research terms, theoretical or construct validity refers to the quality of the relationship between an observation or piece of empirical data collected and the element of the research model that it represents. A related element is that of reliability, which concerns the extent to which the same observational procedure in the same context would yield the same information or observation.

- *Supremacy:* the existence of one universal research method and epistemology (Gable, 1994).

- *Theoretical validity:* see research validity / construct validity

- *Triangulation:* the use of more than one research instrument or method to confirm or deny the evidence from other instrument(s) or method(s).

Relevant Bibliography: Signposts to Further Readings

This book is not an all-encompassing manual for writing research. It is only meant as an easy-to-use shortcut that can help students get to the essentials faster and thus save time in their postgraduate research. We owe much praise and thanks to those who have come before us and who wrote about the long road to research. In this section, we put forward a small sample of very important readings that students will benefit enormously from studying.

Rather than reinventing the wheel and trying to rephrase that which has already been perfectly said, we want to signpost a number of particularly useful articles or books which are easily available and deal in detail with specific aspects of the research process. For each reference, a short description of the content and suggested use is provided.

- Bouchard, T.J. (1976) Field research methods: interviewing, questionnaires, participant observation, systematic observation, unobtrusive measures, in Dunnette (Ed) *Handbook of Organisational and Industrial Psychology*, Rand McNally, Chicago, 363-413.

  A rather complete guide to the field-oriented research methods available to researchers. This chapter argues that there is no substitute for studying human behaviour in real settings as opposed to laboratories. It provides much useful information on interviews as a data collection tool.

- Bryman, A. (1988) *Quantity and Quality in Social Research*, Routledge and Kegan Paul, London, U.K.

  Focusing on the investigations of organisations and what happens in them, this book is an attempt to help students in the management and business areas to apply (translate) the findings of research in sociology and psychology to their own research projects.

- Carlson S. (1951) *Executive Behaviour: A Study of the Work Load and the Working Methods of Managing Directors*, Stronbergs, Stockholm, Sweden.

  We can't resist mentioning this landmark study of top managers' work, which set the standard for research in the management area.

- Checkland, P. (1981) *Systems Thinking – Systems Practice*, Wiley Publications, Chichester, U.K.

  The ultimate reference for systems thinking. This book contains both the historical dimension of systems thinking and the more recent developments of the concept.

- Denzin and Lincoln (1994) (Eds) *Handbook of Qualitative Research*, Sage Publications, London, U.K.

  Very complete collection of articles on the practice of qualitative research by very experienced researchers. Contribution from Guba and Lincoln (on the paradigmatic debate in social sciences), Stake (on case studies) and Miles and Huberman deserve special mention.

- a) Denzin and Lincoln (1998) (Eds) *The Landscape of Qualitative Research Theories and Issues*, Sage Publications, London, U.K.

- b) Denzin and Lincoln (1998) (Eds) *Strategies of Qualitative Enquiry*, Sage Publications, London, U.K.

- c) Denzin and Lincoln (1998) (Eds) *Collecting and Interpreting of Qualitative Materials*, Sage Publications, London, U.K.

  This three-volume paperback version of the 1994 text considers the major strategies employed by qualitative researchers in the first volume; the field of qualitative research is considered from a theoretical perspective in the second volume; and the final volume considers the collecting, analysing and interpreting of qualitative research materials.

- Dubin, R. (1969) *Theory Building*, New York, Free Press.

  The ultimate reference for any researcher who wants to conduct a project with some rigorous theory-building in mind. The problem is that this book is rather long and difficult, but it is also very complete.

- Glaser, B. and Strauss, A. (1967) *The Discovery of Grounded Theory*, Aldine, Chicago.

  This is the original book where grounded theory is being described by its founders. It is mainly focused on their initial studies in a hospital environment and later books might be more relevant to many research projects (see Strauss and Corbin in this list).

- Hart, C. (1998) *Doing a Literature Review*, The Open University, Sage Publications.

  This is a technical manual, particularly relevant to the writing of the review of previous research section of the thesis. As pointed out in the book, writing such sections has become somewhat of a ritual and much time can be saved by drawing on the experience accumulated by others.

- Kaplan, R. (1986) The role of empirical research in management accounting, *Accounting, Organizations and Society*, 11(4/5), 429-452.

  Review of the research methods currently used in management accounting and argumentation for more empirically oriented research in this area, namely, case studies initially and then more specific field studies.

- McGrath, J. E (1984) *Groups – Interaction and Performance*, (1st Edition), Englewood Cliffs, NJ, Prentice-Hall.

  The reference for any student intending on using previous findings in group research. McGrath's synthesis of this body of research covers 100 years of experimentation and is very clearly explained.

- McGrath, J.E., Martin, J. and Kulka, R. (1982) *Judgement Calls in Research*, Beverly Hills, Sage Publications.

  In a less serious mode, this book presents a hyperrealist vision of the research process. The authors attempt to demystify the overly theoretical conception of research as described in textbooks by showing how choices made as a matter of fact by researchers influence the results of their research significantly.

- a) Miles, M. and Huberman, A. (1994) *Qualitative Data Analysis: An Expanded Sourcebook*, Sage Publications, CA.

- b) Miles, M. and Huberman, A. (1984) *Qualitative Data Analysis*: A Sourcebook of New Methods, Sage, Beverly Hills.

  Two editions of essentially the same book (though the 1994 edition is probably better). This book contains invaluable advice on how to present the results of research. The section on the different types of figures and tables that can be used to emphasise the meaning of data is a must.

- Miller, D.C. (1991) *Handbook of Research Design and Social Measurement*, Newbury Park, California, Sage (5th Edition).

  This book, regularly updated, provides a series of quick articles on every conceivable aspects of carrying out research in any area in the social sciences.

- Mintzberg H. (1973) *The Nature of Managerial Work*, Prentice Hall.

  This book is often used as the ultimate reference for research on the work of managers. It must at the very least be regarded as a compulsory starting point for any student wanting to research aspects of managerial work.

- Mintzberg H. (1979) An emerging strategy of "direct" research, *Administrative Science Quarterly*, **24**, 4, 582–589.

  Another key reference to Mintzberg's work where he makes the case for focusing on single, rich case studies.

- Mumford, E. (1985) *Research Methods in Information Systems*, North Holland.

  This book presents the proceedings of the first IFIP 8.1 conference in Manchester (1984). The theme of the conference (research methods in IS research) was quite novel at that time. It contains essential material for any students carrying out research in IS.

- Nissen *et al.* (eds.) (1991) *Information Systems Research: Contemporary Approach and Emergent Traditions*, North Holland.

  This book presents the proceedings of the second IFIP 8.1 conference in Stockholm (1990). It also contains important material for any students carrying out research in IS.

- Nohria and Eccles (eds.) (1992) *Networks and Organisations: Structure Form and Action*, Harvard Business School Press, Boston, MA.

  Unlike other references put forward in this section, this book is not exactly a mainstream research guide. It reports on recent experiment with social network analysis, a mode of research little used outside sociology, but which we see as having great potential for investigations into organisations. The introduction by Nohria sets the scene and demonstrates the potential of this alternative research mode.

- Patton, M. (1990) *Qualitative evaluation and research methods*, Sage Publications, Newbury Park, CA.

  This voluminous book can be used as a reference for many aspects of the research process. In particular, the sections on purposive sampling and on preparing questions for interviews and questionnaires are quite good.

- Perrow, C. (1970) *Organisational Analysis – A Sociological View*, Tavistock Publications.

  This book presents important advice for researchers who study organisations and who try to draw conclusions from what they observe in organisations and to interpret the differences they find between the cases they study.

- Ryan, B., Scapens, R. and Theobald, M. (1992) *Research Methodology in Finance and Accounting*, Academic Press Inc., Harcourt Brace Jovanovich, London.

  A good starting point for students attempting to get to grips with the research traditions in finance, financial accounting and management accounting.

- Strauss, A. and Corbin, J. (1990) *Basics of Qualitative Research: Grounded Theory Procedures and Techniques*, Sage Publications, Newbury Park, CA.

  This book presents a more modern and less radical approach to the application of grounded theory to research in a wide variety of fields. It constitutes a more relaxed vision of the original concept, a vision to which Glaser, the other founding father of grounded theory, does not subscribe. Those who are interested in the shift between Glaser and Strauss can read Glaser, B. (1992) *The Basics of Grounded Theory Analysis: Emergence vs. Forcing*, Sociology Press, Imprint Mill Valley to find out more.

- Van Maanen, J. (1988) *Tales from the Field*, The University of Chicago Press, Chicago.

  This short book draws on the experience accumulated in anthropology to present very pointed and useful remarks on the process of carrying out research. It is particularly relevant for students who intend to carry out qualitative research and deals with the issue of bias in research.

- Weick, K. E. (1979), *The Social Psychology of Organisations* (2nd edition), Addison-Wesley, Reading, MA.

  This book is still a reference for studies on organisations and the behaviour of actors in them. It presents the more philosophical aspects of research on organisations.

- Whyte, W. (1984) *Learning from the Field*, Sage Publications, Newbury Park, CA.

  In this book, William Whyte reports on 50 years of his own experience with carrying out research in a variety of communities and organisations. Some of his chapters contain very useful advice for novice researchers.

- a) Yin, R. (1994) *Case Study Research – Design and Methods, Applied Social Research Methods Series Volume 5*, Sage Publications, London.

- b) Yin, R.K. (1989) *Case Study Research – Design and Methods*, Sage Publications, Newbury Park, CA.

  Two editions of the same book. This is the bible for researchers who want to use case study in a rigorous manner. Can be used in combination with Stake, 1994 (see Denzin and Lincoln in this list) and Miles and Huberman, 1994 (in this list).

- Yin, R. (1993) *Applications of Case Study Research, Applied Social Research Methods Series Volume 34*, Sage Publications, London.

  This presents a sequel to the 1989 edition of the previous text. Chapter three is particularly relevant, as it deals with research design issues in the use of case studies for information systems research.

Letters of Introduction and Non-Disclosure Agreements

There are a number of ways of initiating relations with your chosen research site, depending upon the type of research access necessary and the data required. Conducting a survey represents the simplest form of access once the informants have been correctly identified. Other forms of field inquiry necessitate more deliberate approach strategies. Those most frequently used are discussed below.

Introductory Letter

The letter of introduction you send to your proposed research site represents their first chance to evaluate you and your proposal. Usually, at the level of postgraduate master's dissertation/theses, you will be dealing with an organisation with whom you will either have had previous contacts through your university or college, or alternatively one which has received much publicity relevant in some way to the topic you are studying. Regardless of research strategy, students are best advised to initially contact just one person in an organisation and then enlist the help of this individual in setting up interviews, document access, plant tours, etc. A sample letter is presented on the next page.

Mary Murphy
Post-graduate Room
Dept of Accounting
O'Rahilly Building
University College Cork

Mr Michael O'Connor
MIS Manager
Multitech Limited
John Street
Cork

9th October,

1999
Dear Mr. O'Connor,

My name is Mary Murphy and I am a postgraduate student of the Department of Accounting at University College Cork. I am currently researching the area of Business Process Re-engineering, and further to your telephone conversation with my supervisor, Dr Adam, during this past week, I understand that your organisation is in the process of a re-engineering initiative.

I would like to arrange to discuss with you, at your convenience, the possibility of carrying out some empirical research at your organisation. Please find enclosed a copy of my research proposal outlining the scope of the research project.

Yours sincerely,

_____

Mary Murphy

Some points to note:

- Arrange with your supervisor to print this letter on the headed paper of your department. This improves its presentation and will give your contact more confidence in your ability.

- It always helps to send any correspondence to named individuals within an organisation. It becomes much easier to follow up if you do not receive a reply and also demonstrates some level of initial research has been conducted on the organisation. In the example presented above, Mary has already asked her supervisor to telephone the organisation beforehand, so her letter will be expected.

- Ensure that you have spelled the name of the contact individual and of the organisation correctly and that you have the correct postal address. If you are unsure of a title or an address, you can ring the receptionist in the organisation and simply ask for the information you require.

- The letter should be brief and to the point. At this stage, you do not need to go into elaborate details on your research project. Simply attach a one-page summary, similar to your initial research proposal. Again, you need to use some common sense and ensure that you do not include anything likely to negatively influence the recipient of the letter in their decision whether or not to meet you.

Introductory E-mail

Organisations and people within them are becoming more and more technologically efficient, thus, we have found that it may be easier to contact people electronically. Similar points can be made here as were made regarding the introductory letter. Use of e-mail is, however, slightly more informal. The key points are to keep your mail brief and to the point. Try to explain who you are, what the research is about and why you want to contact that particular person. Send the e-mail to a named individual. Most organisations have some form of web presence, so if you are unsure of the correct e-mail address, simply send the message with a covering message to the web master asking him to forward it to the named individual. This strategy has worked quite successfully for both of the authors of this book in the past.

Cover Letter to Include with a Survey

People in organisations are usually extremely busy, thus, you need to make the process of answering your survey as painless as possibly. Send the survey to named individuals; informants are usually more willing to deal with something that seems to have been directed at them rather than something that has by default / accident landed on their desk.

A covering letter briefly explaining who you are and the purposes of the study to which their response will contribute lends credibility to the questionnaire, particularly if you are able to use the headed paper of your department. Again, you need to keep this letter brief and to the point. You may also wish to offer respondents the opportunity of obtaining copies of the results of the study. If you make this offer, be sure to follow through on positive responses as soon as is practical. Not doing so reflects badly not only on you, but on your department and future students in your course of study who may need the data gathering opportunity such individuals could offer, but may not find it forthcoming if they have had negative prior experiences with such students.

Non-Disclosure Agreement

A non-disclosure document (NDA) is an agreement made between the researcher and his institution and the organisation in which the research is being carried out regarding the specifics of access and of the subsequent use of the research materials gathered. In formalising the terms of the agreement, try to preserve your independence of judgment / conclusion. Many NDAs come in standard form and you are best advised to consult with your supervisor regarding the terms and conditions contained therein.

If you are able to negotiate the terms of the agreement, then you need to consider the following:

- Seek an exploratory meeting with the organisation to discuss possible contributions by the organisation to your research. The organisation may be more favourably disposed towards you if you persuade your supervisor to come along too.

- Nominal disguising of the organisation is acceptable, but full disclosure is ideal. If this is not possible, try (without being too unreasonable) to limit the time to which the agreement applies.

- Offer to comply with the requirements for the next two years, with an agreement to review the NDA after that point. The data may have become less sensitive by then and students wishing to remain in academia will be actively seeking publication possibilities.

- Offer to provide "letters of comfort" from your supervisor/head of department (but ask their permission to do so first!).

Introductory Telephone Contact

As a form of initial contact, novice researchers would be well advised to use the telephone only as a last resort. The written word allows for much more careful consideration as to content and tone. Some pointers regarding telephone contact:

- Think through very clearly what it is you wish to say - you are best advised to explain briefly who you are and what your research project is about. Make sure you can do this in about three or four sentences. Then arrange a meeting to further discuss the project.

- Get the name and exact title of the individual you wish to contact. Do not be surprised, however, if they are unavailable to take your call. Prepare a short, concise message that can be left on a voice mail service or with their administrator.

- If you encounter a voice mail service, remember to leave a contact phone number. If it is the postgraduate lab in your department, warn your fellow postgraduates that you are expecting the return call. Make sure that everyone who may answer the phone at the number you left is aware that industry contacts may ring and that elementary rules of courtesy must be respected at all times.

Dissertation Management Checklist: Mapping the Book to the Practical Experience (Your Personal Odyssey)

The diagram on the next page may help students to organise their research effort and plan for the work ahead. It may also help them in understanding and measuring the effect of not meeting a deadline for the completion date of their projects.

Students should use the short horizontal lines besides the different stages of the project to write down the projected and actual dates of the completion of each stage. At the top of the diagram they should write the start date, which is the only one to be known with certainty. By talking to their supervisors, they can determine what are realistic dates for the completion of each of the major stages until the end of the research project.

As each milestone is reached either within or outside of the allocated time, students can measure the effect on the overall date of completion. This mechanism may seem somewhat trivial, but it is not totally unrealistic in the sense that time lost at the start and along the way will necessarily have an effect on the completion of each of the following stages. Thus, a planned completion date should always be re-examined in view of the deviations between the plan and what really happens. This can be of use for students who go to interviews and are asked when they will be ready to start in their new employment.

The diagram on the next page can be photocopied (and enlarged) and stuck on the wall in a key spot where it will provide additional motivation to students. Feel free to colour in, modify or deface in any manner conducive to your successful completion of the dissertation!

Good luck and keep your head down!

Bibliography

Adam, F. (1996) Experimentation with Organisation Analyser, a tool for the study of decision making networks in organisations in Humphreys, Bannon, McCosh, Migliarese and Pomerol (eds) *Implementing Systems for Supporting Management Decisions*, London: Chapman and Hall, 1– 20.

Adam, F. (1992) *The Identification and Analysis of Information Flows among Senior Executives – An Empirical Study,* Unpublished Masters Thesis, University College Cork, Ireland.

Anthony, R.N. (1965) *Planning and Control Systems: A Framework for Analysis*, Boston: Harvard University Press.

Barker, R., Dembo, T. and Lewin, K. (1941) *Frustration and regression: an experiment with young children*, University of Iowa Studies in Child Welfare, 18, No. 386.

Bonoma, T.V. (1985) Case research in marketing: opportunities, problems and a process, *Journal of Marketing Research*, 22(2), 199–208.

Bouchard, T.J. (1976) Field research methods: interviewing, questionnaires, participant observation, systematic observation, unobtrusive measures, in Dunnette (ed) *Handbook of Organizational and Industrial Psychology*, Chicago: Rand McNally, 363–413.

Boynton, A.C., Zmud R.W. and Jacobs G.C. (1994) The influence of IT management practice on IT use in large organisations, *MIS Quarterly*, 18(3), 299–318.

Brennan, N. (1998) *Accounting Research: A Practical Guide*, Dublin: Oak Tree Press.

Bromwich, M. (1990) The Case for Strategic Management Accounting: The Role of Accounting Information in *Competitive Markets, Accounting, Organizations and Society*, Vol. 15(1/2), 27–46.

Browne, J. (1976) Fieldwork for fun and profit, in Golden (ed) *The Research Experience*, Itasca: Peacock.

Bruns, W. (1989) A Review of Robert Yin's Case Study Research: Design and Methods, *Journal of Management Accounting Research*, Vol. 1, Fall, 157–163.

Bryman, A. (1988) *Quantity and Quality in Social Research*, London: Routledge and Kegan Paul.

Buchler, J. (1955) *Philosophical Writings of Pierce*, New York: Dover.

Burgess, R. (1982) (ed) *Field Research: A Source Book and Field Manual*, London: George Allen & Unwin.

Burrell, G. and Morgan, G. (1979) *Sociological Paradigms and Organisational Analysis*, London: Heinemann.

Burt, R. (1992) The social structure of competition, in Nohria and Eccles (eds) *Networks and Organisations: Structure Form and Action*, Boston: Harvard Business School Press, 57–90.

Carlson, S. (1951) *Executive Behaviour: A Study of The Work Load and the Working Methods of Managing Directors*, Stockholm: Stronbergs.

Checkland, P. (1981) *Systems Thinking – Systems Practice*, Chicester: Wiley Publications.

Ciborra, C. (1988) Knowledge and Systems in Organisations: A Typology and Proposal, in Lee, McCosh and Migliarese, P. (eds) *Organisational Decision Support Systems*, Amsterdam: North Holland Elsevier, 220–245.

Cohen, D., March, J.G. and Olsen, J.P. (1972) A garbage can model of organisational choice, *Administrative Science Quarterly*, 17, 1–25.

Coulson-Thomas, C.J. (1994) *Business Process Re-engineering: Myth or Reality*, London: Kogan Page.

Daft, R.L. and Lengel, R.H. (1986) Organisational information requirements media richness and structural design, *Management Science*, 32(5), 554–571.

Daft, R., Lengel, R. and Trevino L. (1987) Message equivocality media selection and manager performance: implications for information systems, *MIS Quarterly*, 11, 355–366.

Daft, R., Parks, D. and Sormunen, J. (1988) Chief executive scanning environmental characteristics and company performance: an empirical study, *Strategic Management Journal*, 9, 123–139.

Daft, R. and Weick, K.E. (1984) Toward a Model of Organisations as Interpretations Systems, *Academy of Management Review*, 9, 284–295.

Daft, R.L. and Lengel, R.H. (1984) Information richness: a new approach to managerial behaviour and organisation design, *Research in Organisational Behaviour*, 6, 191–233.

de Vaus, D.A. (1994) *Surveys in Social Research*, 3rd edition, London: UCL Press.

Deasy, C. (1999) *Developing a Performance Measurement System for Strategy Implementation and Formulation – A Critical Success Factor-based Approach,* Unpublished Masters Thesis, University College Cork, Ireland.

Dent, J. (1990) Strategy, Organisation and Control: Some Possibilities for Accounting Research, *Accounting, Organizations and Society*, Vol. 15 (1/2) 3–25.

Denzin, N. and Lincoln, Y. (1998) (eds) *Collecting and Interpreting of Qualitative Materials*, London: Sage Publications.

Denzin, N. and Lincoln, Y. (1998) (eds) *Strategies of Qualitative Enquiry*, London: Sage Publications.

Denzin, N. and Lincoln, Y. (1998) (eds) *The Landscape of Qualitative Research Theories and Issues*, London: Sage Publications.

Denzin, N. and Lincoln, Y. (1994) (eds) *Handbook of Qualitative Research*, London: Sage Publications.

Dumont, R.G. and Wilson, W.J. (1967) Aspects of concept formation, explication, and theory construction in sociology, *American Sociological*

Review, 32, 985–95.

Dubin, R. (1969) *Theory and Building*, New York: Free Press.

Dunnette, C. (1976) *The Handbook of Organisational and Industrial Psychology*, Chicago: Rand McNally.

Earl, M.J. (1989), *Management Strategies for Information Technologies*, New York: Prentice-Hall.

Earl, M.J. and Hopwood, A.G. (1980) From management information to information management, in Lucas, Land, Lincoln and Supper (eds) *The Information Systems Environment*, North-Holland, IFIP, 1980, 133–143.

Earl, M.J. (1992) Putting IT in its place: a polemic for the nineties, *Journal of Information Technology*, 7, 100–108.

Eisenhardt, K.M. (1989) Making fast decisions in high velocity environments, *Academy of Management Journal*, 32(3), 543–576.

Eisenhardt, K.M. (1990) Speed and strategic choice: how managers accelerate decision making, *California Management Review*, 31, 39–54.

Fahy, M. and Murphy, C. (1996) From end user computing to management developed systems in Dias Cuehlo *et al.* (eds) *Proceedings of the Fourth European Conference on Information Systems*, Lisbon, Portugal, July 1996, 127–142.

Fawl, C.L. (1963) Disturbances experienced by children in their natural habitats, in Barker (ed) *The Stream of Behaviour*, New York: Aleton-Century-Crofts.

Fayol, H. (1916) *General And Industrial Management*, London: Pitman.

Fitzgerald, B. (1997) *Methodology-in-Action: the Nature of Usage of Systems Development Methodologies in Practice*, Unpublished Ph.D. Thesis, University of London, Birbeck College.

Fitzgerald, B. (1998) An empirical investigation into the adoption of systems development methodologies, *Information and Management*, 34, 317–328.

Fitzgerald, B. and Howcroft, D. (1997) *Towards Dissolution of the IS Research Debate: From Polarisation to Polarity*, ESRC Discussion Paper, Cork, REF: 97/5.

Gable, G. (1994) Integrating Case Study and Survey Research Methods: An Example in Information Systems, *European Journal of Information Systems*, Vol. 3(2), 112–126.

Galliers, R. and Land, F. (1987) Choosing appropriate information systems research methodologies, *Communication of the ACM*, 30(11), 900–902.

Galliers, R.D. (1985) In search of a paradigm for information systems research, in Mumford *et al.* (eds) *Research Methods in Information Systems*, North Holland.

Gartell, B. (1979) Is ethnography possible? A critique of African odyssey, *Journal of Anthropological Studies*, 35(4), 424–446.

Giddens, A. (1976) *New Rules of Sociological Method*, New York: Basic Books.

Glaser, B. (1992) *The Basics of Grounded Theory Analysis: Emergence vs.*

Forcing, Imprint Mill Valley: Sociology Press.

Glaser, B. and Strauss, A. (1967) *The Discovery of Grounded Theory*, Chicago: Aldine.

Gorry, A. and Scott Morton, M. (1971) A Framework for Management Information Systems, *Sloan Management Review*, Fall, 55–70.

Granovetter, M.S. (1973) The strength of weak ties, *American Journal of Sociology*, 78, 1360–1380.

Guba, E.G. and Lincoln, Y.S. (1994) Competing paradigms in qualitative research in Denzin and Lincoln (eds) *Handbook of Qualitative Research*, London: Sage Publications, 105–117.

Gulden, G. and Ewers, D. (1989) Is Your ESS Meeting the Need? *Computerworld* July 10, 85–91.

Guss, C.L. (1999) The Virtual Project Environment and Success – Research and Results, *Virtual-Organisation*, 2(3), 21–28.

Hakim, C. (1987) Research Design: Strategies and Choices in the Design of Social Research, *Contemporary Social Research Studies Series*, No. 13, Allen & Unwin.

Hammer, M. and Champy, J. (1993) *Re-engineering the Corporation: A Manifesto for Business Revolution*, London: Nicholas Brealey Publishing.

Hart, C. (1998) *Doing a Literature Review*, The Open University, Sage Publications.

Healy, M. (1995) *An Empirical Investigation of Business Process Re-engineering as a Mechanism for Change*, Unpublished Masters Thesis, University College Cork, Ireland.

Hickson, D.J., Butler, R.J., Cray, D., Mallory, D. and Wilson, D.C. (1985) Comparing 150 decision processes, in Pennings *et al.* (eds) *Organisational Strategy and Change*, London: Jossey-Bass Publishers.

Hirschheim, R.A. (1985) Information systems epistemology: an historical perspective in Mumford *et al.* (eds) *Research Methods in Information Systems*, North Holland, 28–60.

Hopwood, A. (1983) On trying to study accounting in the contexts in which it operates, *Accounting, Organizations and Society*, Vol. 8(2/3), 287–305.

Howel, R. and Soucy, S. (1990) Customer Profitability – As Critical as Product Profitability, *Management Accounting*, October, 43–47.

Hughes, J.A. (1976) *Sociological Analysis: Methods of Discovery*, London: Nelson.

Jayson, S. (1992) Focus on People – Not Costs, *Management Accounting*, September, 42–47.

Jenkins, M. (1985) Research methodologies and MIS research in Mumford *et al.* (eds) *Research Methods in Information Systems*, North Holland, 103–117.

Jick, T. (1979) Mixing Qualitative and Quantitative Methods: Triangulation in Action, *Administrative Science Quarterly*, 24, 602–611.

Johnson, H.T. and Kaplan, R.S. (1987) *Relevance Lost – The Rise and Fall of Management Accounting Research,* Boston: Harvard Business School Press.

Jones, J., Saunders, C. and McLeod, R. (1988) Information media and source patterns across management levels: A pilot study, *Journal of Management Information Systems*, 5(3), 71–84.

Jones, J., Saunders, C. and McLeod, R. (1993) Media usage and velocity in executive information acquisition, *European Journal of Information Systems,* 2(4), 260–271.

Jones, J.W. and McLeod, R. (1986) The structure of executive information systems: an exploratory analysis, *Decision Sciences*, 17, 220–249.

Kaplan, B. and Duchon, D. (1988) Combining qualitative and quantitative methods in information systems research: a case study, *Management Information Systems Quarterly*, 12(4), 571–586.

Kaplan, R. (1986) The role of empirical research in management accounting, *Accounting, Organizations and Society,* 11(4/5), 429–452.

Kaplan, R. (1993) Research Opportunities in Management Accounting, *Journal of Management Accounting Research*, Fall, 1–4.

Kerlinger, F.N. (1973) *Foundations of Behavioural Research*, London: Holt-Saunders International Editions.

Kotter, J. (1984) What effective managers really do, *Harvard Business Review*, November/December, 156–167.

Kraemer, K. and Dutton, W. (1991) Survey research on information systems, in Kraemer (ed) *The Information Systems Challenge: Survey Research Methods*, Publishing Division, Boston: Harvard Business School, Vol. 3, 3–57.

Kulka, R.A. (1982) Idiosyncrasy and circumstance: choices and constraints in the research process in McGrath, Martin, and Kulka (eds) *Judgement Calls in Research,* Beverly Hills: Sage Publications, 41–69.

Langley, A., Mintzberg, N., Pitcher, P., Posada, E. and Saint-Macauly, J. (1995) Opening up Decision Making: The View from the Black Stool, *Organisational Science* 6(3), May–June, 260–279.

Layder, D. (1993) *Strategies in Social Research*, Polity Press.

Lee, A.S. (1991) Integrating positivist and interpretive approaches to organisational research, *Organization Science*, 2, 342–365.

Lewis, O. (1951) *Life in a Mexican Village: Tepoztlan Restudied*, Urbana: University of Illinois Press.

Lincoln, Y. and Guba, E. (1985) *Naturalistic Inquiry*, Beverly Hills: Sage Publications.

Luthans, F. and Davis, T.R.V. (1982) An idiographic approach to organisational behaviour research: the use of single case experimental designs and direct measures, *Academy of Management Review*, 7(3), 380–391.

March, J. and Simon, H. (1993), *Organisations*, 2nd edition, Cambridge: Blackwell Publishers.

Marshall, C. and Rossman, G. (1989), *Designing Qualitative Research*, Beverly Hills: Sage Publications.

Martin, J. (1982) A garbage can model of the research process, in McGrath,

Martin and Kulka (eds) *Judgment Calls in Research*, Beverly Hills: Sage Publications, 17–40.

Martindale, D. (1974) *Sociological Theory and the Problem of Values*, Columbus: Charles E. Merrill.

McGrath, J.E. (1984) *Groups – Interaction and Performance*, 1st edition, Englewood Cliffs: Prentice-Hall.

McGrath, J.E. (1982) Dilemmatics; the study of research choices and dilemmas in McGrath, Martin and Kulka (eds) *Judgement Calls in Research*, Beverly Hills: Sage Publications, 69–102.

McGrath, J.E., Martin, J. and Kulka, R.A. (1982) Some quasi-rules for making judgement calls in research in McGrath, Martin and Kulka (eds) *Judgement Calls in Research*, Beverly Hills: Sage Publications, 103–118.

McGrath, J.E., Martin, J. and Kulka, R. (1982) *Judgement Calls in Research*, Beverly Hills: Sage Publications.

McLeod, R. and Jones, J. (1986) Making Executive Information Systems more efficient, *Business Horizons*, September-October, 53–69.

McLeod, R., Jones, J. and Poitevent, J. (1984) Executives' perceptions of their information sources, *Proceedings of the 4th International Conference on DSS*, Dallas, April 1984.

Miles, M. and Huberman, A. (1984) *Qualitative Data Analysis: A Sourcebook of New Methods*, Beverly Hills: Sage Publications.

Miles, M. and Huberman, A. (1994) *Qualitative Data Analysis: an Expanded Sourcebook*, Beverly Hills: Sage Publications.

Miller, D. (1991) *Handbook of Research Design and Social Measurement*, 5th edition, Beverly Hills: Sage Publications.

Mintzberg, H. (1973) *The Nature of Managerial Work*, Englewood Cliffs: Prentice Hall.

Mintzberg, H. (1978) Patterns in Strategy Formation, *Management Science*, Vol. 24 (9), 934–938.

Mintzberg, H. (1985) A Grass Roots Model of Strategy Formation, *Administrative Science Quarterly*, June, 305–385.

Mintzberg, H., Raisinghani, D. and Theoret, A. (1976) The Structure of Unstructured Decision Processes, *Administrative Science Quarterly*, 21, 246–275.

Moore, R. (1977) Becoming a sociologist in Parkwood, Bell and Newby (eds) *Doing Sociological Research*, New York: Macmillan.

Mumford, E, (1985) *Research Methods in Information Systems*, North Holland.

Nissen, H., Klein, H. and Hirschheim, R. (eds) (1991) *Information Systems Research: Contemporary Approach and Emergent Traditions*, North Holland: Elsevier Publishers.

Nohria N. and Eccles R. (1992) *Networks and Organisations: Structure Form and Action*, Boston: Harvard Business School Press.

Nonaka, I. (1991) The Knowledge-Creating Company, *Harvard Business Review*, November-December, 97–104.

Oppenheim, A. (1996) *Questionnaire Design and Attitude Measurement*, London: Heinemann.

Otley, D. (1988) Behavioural and Organisational Research in Management Accounting in Cooper, D., Scapens, R. and Arnold J. (eds) *Management Accounting Research and Practice*, CIMA Occasional Papers, 136–158.

Patton, M. (1990) *Qualitative evaluation and research methods*, Newbury Park: Sage Publications.

Perrow, C. (1970) *Organisational Analysis: A Sociological View*, London: Tavistock Publications.

Poloma, M. (1979) *Contemporary Sociological Theory*, New York: MacMillan.

Porter, M.E. and Millar, V.E. (1985) How information can give you competitive advantage, *Harvard Business Review*, July/August, 149–160.

Pounds, W. (1969) The Process of problem-finding, *Industrial Management Review*, 11(1), 1–19.

Redfield, R. (1930) *Tepoztlan: a Mexican village,* Chicago: University of Chicago Press.

Rockset, J. and van Bullen, C. (1985) *The Rise of Management Computing*, Homewood, Il: Dow Jones Irwin.

Rubin, H. and Rubin, I. (1995) *Qualitative Interviewing: The Art of Hearing,* Beverly Hills: Sage Publications.

Rudner, R.S. (1966) *Philosophy of Social Science*, Englewood Cliffs: Prentice-Hall.

Ryan, B., Scapens, R. and Theobald, M. (1992) *Research Method and Methodology*, Academic Press.

Sauer, C.H. (1993) *Why Information Systems Fail: A Case Study Approach*, Henley-On-Thames: Alfred Waller.

Schwandt, T.A. (1994) Constructivist, interpretivist approaches to human inquiry in Denzin and Lincoln (eds) *Handbook of Qualitative Research*, London: Sage Publications, 118–137.

Sellitz, C., Jahoda, H., Deutsch, M. and Cook, S. (1967) *Research Methods on Social Relations*, Metheun & Co. Ltd.

Shaffir, W. and Stebbins, R. (1991) (eds) *Experiencing Fieldwork - An inside view of qualitative research*, Beverly Hills: Sage Publications.

Simmonds, K. (1981), Strategic Management Accounting in Fanning, D. (ed) (1983), *Handbook of Management Accounting*, Gower Publishing Co., 25–48.

Simon, H. (1977) *The New Science of Management Decisions,* Englewood Cliffs: Prentice Hall.

Simon, H.A. (1957) *Administrative Behaviour*, New York: Macmillan Company.

Simon, H.A. (1957) *Models of Man,* New York: John Wiley & Sons Inc.

Simon, H.A. (1980) The behavioural and social sciences, *Science*, July, 72–78.

Slater, M.K. (1976) *African Odyssey: an Anthropological Adventure,* Garden City, NY: Anchor.

Stake, R.E. (1994) Case studies, in Denzin and Lincoln (eds) *Handbook of Qualitative Research*, London: Sage Publications.

Stewart R. (1967) *Managers and Their Jobs*, London: Macmillan.

Strassmann, P. (1994) The Rap on Re-engineering, *Computerworld*, Vol. 28 (39), 26th September, 119–121.

Strauss, A. and Corbin, J. (1990) *Basics of Qualitative Research: Grounded Theory Procedures and Techniques*, Newbury Park: Sage Publications.

Strauss, A.L. (1987) *Qualitative Analysis for Social Scientists,* Cambridge University Press.

Street, D., Vinter, R. and Perrow, C. (1966) *Organisation for Treatment*, New York: Free Press.

Todorov, T. (1989) *Nous et les Autres*, Edition du Seuil, Paris.

Trigg, R. (1985) *Understanding Social Science*, New York: Basil Blackwell.

Trow, M. (1957) Comments on 'Participant observation' and 'interviewing': a comparison, *Human Organisation*, 16, 33–35.

Van Maanen, J. (1983) *Qualitative Methodology*, Beverly Hills: Sage Publications.

Vitale, M., Ives, B. and Beath, C. (1986) Linking information technology and corporate strategy: an organisational view, *Proceedings of the First International Conference on Information Technology,* 265–274.

Walker, R. (1985) *Applied Qualitative Research*, Aldershot, England: Gower Publishing Company, Gower House.

Wallace, R. and Mellor, C. (1988) Non-response bias in mail accounting surveys: a pedagogical note, *British Accounting Review*, 20(2), 131–139.

Ward, J. and Griffiths, P. (1996) *Strategic Planning for Information Systems*, Chichester: Wiley and Sons.

Webster's College Dictionary (1990) Random House.

Weick, K.E. (1979) *The Social Psychology of Organisations*, 2nd edition, Reading: Addison-Wesley.

Weick, K. (1984), Theoretical Assumptions and Research Methodology Selection, in McFarlan, W. (ed) *The Information Systems Research Challenge*, Boston: Harvard Business School Press.

Whitehead, A. (1911) *An Introduction to Mathematics,* New York: Holt, Rinehart & Winston.

Whyte, W. (1984) *Learning from the Field*, Newbury Park: Sage Publications.

Wilson, R. (1994) Competitor Analysis, *Management Accounting* (UK) April, 24–25.

Wolcott, H.F. (1982) Differing styles of on-site research, or, if it isn't ethnography, what is it?, *Review Journal of Philosophy and Social Science*, 7(1/2), 154–169.

Wruck, K. (1994) Financial Policy, Internal Control and Performance – Sealed Air Corporation's Leveraged Special Dividend, *Journal of Financial Economics*, (36) 157–192.

Yin, R. (1993) *Applications of Case Study Research*, Applied Social Research Methods Series, London: Sage Publications, Vol. 34.

Yin, R. (1994) *Case Study Research – Design and Methods*, Applied Social Research Methods Series, London: Sage Publications.

Yin, R.K. (1991) *Applications of Case Study Research*, Washington DC: Cosmos Corporation.

Yin, R.K. (1989) *Case Study Research – Design and Methods*, Newbury Park: Sage Publications.

Zuboff, S. (1988) *In the Age of the Smart Machine*, New York: Basic Books.